SRA
Read to Achieve

Comprehending
Content-Area Text

Workbook

Nancy Marchand-Martella
Ronald Martella

McGraw
Hill
Education

Acknowledgments

The authors thank Michael Milone, Ph.D., Assessment Specialist, for his help in preparing the standardized-test-practice materials.

Photo Credits

Cover photo: mwookie/Peter Galbraith/iStock/Getty Images

mheducation.com/prek-12

Send all inquiries to:
McGraw-Hill Education
8787 Orion Place
Columbus, OH 43240

ISBN: 978-0-07-621990-2
MHID: 0-07-621990-9

Printed in the United States of America.

13 14 15 16 17 QVS 21 22 20 19 18

Contents

Contents

✦ Contents

Lesson 1

Fluency Sample

Name _____ Date _____

Check box: ☐ = Cold Timing ☐ = Hot Timing

	Word Count

Dian Fossey

	2
Dian Fossey was a famous scientist who studied mountain gorillas.	12
She had been interested in animals her whole life. She went to college as a	27
preveterinary student. But then Fossey changed her major to occupational	37
therapy so she could help people learn to live and work independently.	49
Fossey worked for many years as an occupational therapist.	58
Fossey became interested in gorillas after she read a book about them by	71
a zoologist. A zoologist is a scientist who studies animals. Fossey traveled	83
to Africa and spent six weeks there. While in Africa, she met Dr. Louis	97
Leakey, a famous scientist, who later asked her to return to Africa to study	111
gorillas. Fossey agreed. Her life would forever be changed.	120
Fossey lived among the gorillas for almost eighteen years. She spent	131
countless hours watching the gorillas, living among them, and imitating	141
their behaviors and sounds so she could earn their trust. Fossey was	153
so interested in gorillas she studied about them intensely, earning her	164
doctorate from Cambridge University in 1976. She later became a professor	175
at Cornell University and wrote a book about her experiences, *Gorillas in*	187
the Mist. This book is one of the best-selling books about gorillas of all	201
time. In fact, the book was so popular it became a movie.	213
One day, when a gorilla touched Fossey's hand, she became the first	225
known person ever to have voluntary contact with a gorilla. She became	237
very close to one gorilla. She named this gorilla Digit. Fossey watched	249
Digit grow, and the two of them became very close. Digit was later killed	263
by poachers. Poachers are people who kill animals that are endangered	274
or that live on protected land. Fossey was so upset over Digit's death she	288
developed the Digit Fund (now called the Dian Fossey Gorilla Fund) to	300
raise money for the protection of gorillas.	307
In 1985, Fossey was killed. Her death is still considered an unsolved	319
mystery. Her dream was to preserve the safety of gorillas and to watch	332
their numbers grow.	335

Total Words Read	
Total Errors —	
Correct Words per Minute (CWPM) =	

Lesson
2

Text-Connections Chart

Name _____ Date _____

1

What's the topic of the lesson? _____

_____

_____

2

What's your purpose for reading? _____

_____

_____

3

What do you know about the topic? _____

_____

_____

_____

_____

_____

_____

_____

_____

_____

_____

Lesson 2

Decoding-Multipart-Words Strategy

Name _____ Date _____

Strategy Steps

Step 1: Underline all the vowel sounds.

Step 2: Make a slash between the word parts so each part has one vowel sound.

Step 3: Go back to the beginning of the word, and read the parts in order.

Step 4: Read the whole word.

• •

Word 1

Word 2

Lesson 2

Fluency Practice: Decoding Multipart Words

Name _____ Date _____

Jane Goodall

Jane Goodall is one of the most famous scientists in the world. She studies chimpanzees at the Gombe National Reserve in Tanzania, Africa. Goodall's research has shown that we share many things with chimpanzees. For example, she found that about 98 percent of our DNA is the same as the DNA found in chimpanzees. Chimpanzees show emotions and make and use tools. Chimpanzees greet one another with a touch or a kiss, and they eat meat and plants. Goodall observed how chimpanzees gather bugs to eat. They use plant stems or long blades of grass to drag termites out of termite mounds. Goodall learned these important facts while observing these animals for many years. She was able to draw important conclusions about chimpanzees.

During her time in Africa, Goodall made many surprising observations. At first the chimpanzees would not let her near them. Over time the chimpanzees learned to trust her. This trust allowed Goodall to observe behaviors other humans had never observed before. For example, Goodall saw one chimp eating a baby pig. Before this time, chimps were thought to eat only plants. Scientists thought chimps were herbivores. Goodall learned that chimps are in fact omnivores. Omnivores eat both plants and animals. She found that chimps are more like humans than scientists had thought.

Goodall's study of chimpanzees earned her a doctoral degree from Cambridge University in England. In fact, Goodall is one of only a few people to earn a doctorate without first earning her undergraduate degree. Goodall's research was very timely and important.

However, other scientists have criticized Goodall's work. Some scientists said her use of names for the chimpanzees was not a good idea. These scientists claimed that people cannot be totally objective if they name their subjects. These scientists said numbers, not names, should be used when describing the animals in Goodall's research. Goodall said naming the chimpanzees helped her to have a closer bond with them.

Strategy Steps

Step 1: Underline all the vowel sounds.

Step 2: Make a slash between the word parts so each part has one vowel sound.

Step 3: Go back to the beginning of the word, and read the parts in order.

Step 4: Read the whole word.

Word 1 | _____

Word 2 | _____

Text-Connections Chart

Name _____ Date _____

1

What's the topic of the lesson? _____

_____

_____

2

What's your purpose for reading? _____

_____

_____

3

What do you know about the topic? _____

_____

_____

_____

_____

_____

_____

_____

_____

Lesson
3

Decoding-Multipart-Words Strategy

Name _____ Date _____

Strategy Steps

Step 1: Underline all the vowel sounds.

Step 2: Make a slash between the word parts so each part has one vowel sound.

Step 3: Go back to the beginning of the word, and read the parts in order.

Step 4: Read the whole word.

Word 1

Word 2

Lesson 4

Text-Connections Chart

Name _____ Date _____

1

What's the topic of the lesson? _____

_____

_____

2

What's your purpose for reading? _____

_____

_____

3

What do you know about the topic? _____

_____

_____

_____

_____

_____

_____

_____

_____

Lesson

4

Decoding-Multipart-Words Strategy

Name _____ Date _____

Strategy Steps

Step 1: Underline all the vowel sounds.

Step 2: Make a slash between the word parts so each part has one vowel sound.

Step 3: Go back to the beginning of the word, and read the parts in order.

Step 4: Read the whole word.

Word 1

Word 2

Lesson 4

Fluency Practice: Information Learned

Name _____ Date _____

Jane Goodall

Jane Goodall is one of the most famous scientists in the world. She studies chimpanzees at the Gombe National Reserve in Tanzania, Africa. Goodall's research has shown that we share many things with chimpanzees. For example, she found that about 98 percent of our DNA is the same as the DNA found in chimpanzees. Chimpanzees show emotions and make and use tools. Chimpanzees greet one another with a touch or a kiss, and they eat meat and plants. Goodall observed how chimpanzees gather bugs to eat. They use plant stems or long blades of grass to drag termites out of termite mounds. Goodall learned these important facts while observing these animals for many years. She was able to draw important conclusions about chimpanzees.

During her time in Africa, Goodall made many surprising observations. At first the chimpanzees would not let her near them. Over time the chimpanzees learned to trust her. This trust allowed Goodall to observe behaviors other humans had never observed before. For example, Goodall saw one chimp eating a baby pig. Before this time, chimps were thought to eat only plants. Scientists thought chimps were herbivores. Goodall learned that chimps are in fact omnivores. Omnivores eat both plants and animals. She found that chimps are more like humans than scientists had thought.

Goodall's study of chimpanzees earned her a doctoral degree from Cambridge University in England. In fact, Goodall is one of only a few people to earn a doctorate without first earning her undergraduate degree. Goodall's research was very timely and important.

However, other scientists have criticized Goodall's work. Some scientists said her use of names for the chimpanzees was not a good idea. These scientists claimed that people cannot be totally objective if they name their subjects. These scientists said numbers, not names, should be used when describing the animals in Goodall's research. Goodall said naming the chimpanzees helped her to have a closer bond with them.

Directions: Write three things you learned after reading the fluency passage.

1. I learned _____

_____

2. I learned _____

_____

3. I learned _____

_____

Lesson 5

Think-Pair-Share

Name _____ Date _____

Directions: Use the Think-Pair-Share Strategy to complete the question below.

Step 1: **Think** about the question for one minute.

Step 2: **Pair** and complete the question with your partner.

Step 3: **Share** what you wrote with the class.

- -

Suppose you're a scientist studying dog behavior. *Apply* your knowledge of theories to write a theory about why dogs act as they do. Defend your answer.

Text-Connections Chart

Name _____ Date _____

1

What's the topic of the lesson? _____

_____

_____

2

What's your purpose for reading? _____

_____

_____

3

What do you know about the topic? _____

_____

_____

_____

_____

_____

_____

_____

_____

_____

Lesson
1

Context-Clues Strategy

Name _____ Date _____

Decoding-Multipart-Words Strategy

Step 1: Underline all the vowel sounds.

Step 2: Make a slash between the word parts so each part has one vowel sound.

Step 3: Go back to the beginning of the word, and read the parts in order.

Step 4: Read the whole word.

Word

Context-Clues Strategy

When you come across a word you don't know,

Step 1: Read the sentence containing the word.

Step 2: Look for a definition or for examples of the word in the sentence.

Step 3: Read before or after the sentence for a definition or for examples of the word.

Word Meaning from Context

Text-Connections Chart

Name _____ Date _____

1

What's the topic of the lesson? _____

_____

_____

2

What's your purpose for reading? _____

_____

_____

3

What do you know about the topic? _____

_____

_____

_____

_____

_____

_____

_____

_____

Lesson 2

Context-Clues Strategy

Name _____ Date _____

Decoding-Multipart-Words Strategy

Step 1: Underline all the vowel sounds.

Step 2: Make a slash between the word parts so each part has one vowel sound.

Step 3: Go back to the beginning of the word, and read the parts in order.

Step 4: Read the whole word.

Word

Context-Clues Strategy

When you come across a word you don't know,

Step 1: Read the sentence containing the word.

Step 2: Look for a definition or for examples of the word in the sentence.

Step 3: Read before or after the sentence for a definition or for examples of the word.

Word Meaning from Context

Fluency Practice: Decoding Multipart Words

Name _____ Date _____

The Basics of Bird Flu

Bird flu is an infection caused by a virus. Bird flu is also called avian flu. It occurs naturally in birds, but most wild birds don't become sick from it. It spreads easily to domestic birds. Chickens, turkeys, and geese can become quite ill. In rare cases, humans can catch the disease from infected birds. Millions of birds and several humans have died from bird flu.

How the Virus Spreads

Strains of the bird flu virus are often carried by ducks and other waterbirds. These birds pass the virus to other birds. The virus spreads through saliva, mucus, and airborne particles. The virus can be carried on tractors, cages, and clothing. Outdoor markets full of birds and people are a good place for spreading the disease. People who have contact with sick birds may become infected. One infected person may spread the disease to another person.

Symptoms and Treatments

Bird flu symptoms are like those of the common flu. They are cough, fever, muscle pain, and sore throat. People infected with a weak strain of the virus may have only a mild eye infection. People infected with a powerful strain may develop serious respiratory problems. Lung problems are the most common cause of death in patients.

The Federal Drug Administration has approved four drugs for the treatment of bird flu. However, viruses can change their genetic makeup. They may become resistant to the drugs. Then the drugs will no longer work.

Prevention

There is now a vaccine to protect against the most dangerous strain of bird flu. So far, it seems to be working. However, scientists worry that someday the virus may become immune to this vaccine. The first defense against avian flu is to avoid travel to regions where outbreaks have occurred. Here's what you can do to prevent the spread of the disease. Wash your hands often. Don't eat raw eggs. Be sure the poultry you eat is fully cooked. These steps will help keep you safe.

Strategy Steps

Step 1: Underline all the vowel sounds.

Step 2: Make a slash between the word parts so each part has one vowel sound.

Step 3: Go back to the beginning of the word, and read the parts in order.

Step 4: Read the whole word.

Word 1

Word 2

Lesson 3

Text-Connections Chart

Name _____ Date _____

1

What's the topic of the lesson? _____
_____
_____

2

What's your purpose for reading? _____
_____
_____

3

What do you know about the topic? _____
_____
_____
_____
_____
_____
_____
_____
_____
_____

Context-Clues Strategy

Name _____ Date _____

Decoding-Multipart-Words Strategy

Step 1: Underline all the vowel sounds.

Step 2: Make a slash between the word parts so each part has one vowel sound.

Step 3: Go back to the beginning of the word, and read the parts in order.

Step 4: Read the whole word.

Word

Context-Clues Strategy

When you come across a word you don't know,

Step 1: Read the sentence containing the word.

Step 2: Look for a definition or for examples of the word in the sentence.

Step 3: Read before or after the sentence for a definition or for examples of the word.

Word Meaning from Context

Fluency Practice: Standardized Test

Name _____ Date _____

The Basics of Bird Flu

Bird flu is an infection caused by a virus. Bird flu is also called avian flu. It occurs naturally in birds, but most wild birds don't become sick from it. It spreads easily to domestic birds. Chickens, turkeys, and geese can become quite ill. In rare cases, humans can catch the disease from infected birds. Millions of birds and several humans have died from bird flu.

How the Virus Spreads

Strains of the bird flu virus are often carried by ducks and other waterbirds. These birds pass the virus to other birds. The virus spreads through saliva, mucus, and airborne particles. The virus can be carried on tractors, cages, and clothing. Outdoor markets full of birds and people are a good place for spreading the disease. People who have contact with sick birds may become infected. One infected person may spread the disease to another person.

Symptoms and Treatments

Bird flu symptoms are like those of the common flu. They are cough, fever, muscle pain, and sore throat. People infected with a weak strain of the virus may have only a mild eye infection. People infected with a powerful strain may develop serious respiratory problems. Lung problems are the most common cause of death in patients.

The Federal Drug Administration has approved four drugs for the treatment of bird flu. However, viruses can change their genetic makeup. They may become resistant to the drugs. Then the drugs will no longer work.

Prevention

There is now a vaccine to protect against the most dangerous strain of bird flu. So far, it seems to be working. However, scientists worry that someday the virus may become immune to this vaccine. The first defense against avian flu is to avoid travel to regions where outbreaks have occurred. Here's what you can do to prevent the spread of the disease. Wash your hands often. Don't eat raw eggs. Be sure the poultry you eat is fully cooked. These steps will help keep you safe.

Score _____ /8 = _____ %

Directions: Take turns reading the questions. Answer the questions together.

Level 1: "Remember" Questions—each worth 1 point

For Level 1 questions, fill in the space next to the correct answer in your own Workbook.

1. Bird, or avian, flu is an infection caused by what?
   ○ a. Bacteria
   ○ b. A lack of clean water
   ○ c. A virus
   ○ d. Mosquitoes

Lesson 3

Fluency Practice: Standardized Test, continued

Name _____ Date _____

2. How many birds have died from avian flu?
   ○ a. Thousands
   ○ b. Millions
   ○ c. Hundreds
   ○ d. Billions

3. Bird flu spreads to other birds and humans through
   ○ a. saliva.
   ○ b. airborne particles.
   ○ c. mucus.
   ○ d. All of the above

4. People infected with a powerful strain of bird flu may experience what symptoms?
   ○ a. Serious respiratory problems
   ○ b. Skin rash
   ○ c. Heart problems
   ○ d. Severe headaches

5. What happens when viruses change their genetic makeup and become resistant to prescription drugs?
   ○ a. The drugs no longer work to protect against the viruses.
   ○ b. The drugs become "supercharged" to protect against the viruses.
   ○ c. The drugs become more difficult to administer.
   ○ d. The drugs continue to be effective.

6. What is one way you avoid avian flu?
   ○ a. Travel to regions where outbreaks have occurred.
   ○ b. Don't wash your hands.
   ○ c. Don't eat poultry that isn't fully cooked.
   ○ d. Eat raw eggs.

Level 2: "Understand" Question—worth 2 points (2 points for correct answer, 1 point for partially correct answer, 0 points for incorrect answer)

For the Level 2 question, write the answer in the space provided in your own Workbook.

7. Describe two ways bird flu can spread or be carried from person to person.

_____

_____

_____

Lesson 4

Text-Connections Chart

Name _____ Date _____

1

What's the topic of the lesson? _____

_____

_____

2

What's your purpose for reading? _____

_____

_____

3

What do you know about the topic? _____

_____

_____

_____

_____

_____

_____

_____

_____

_____

_____

Lesson 4

Context-Clues Strategy

Name _____ Date _____

Decoding-Multipart-Words Strategy

Step 1: Underline all the vowel sounds.

Step 2: Make a slash between the word parts so each part has one vowel sound.

Step 3: Go back to the beginning of the word, and read the parts in order.

Step 4: Read the whole word.

Word

Context-Clues Strategy

When you come across a word you don't know,

Step 1: Read the sentence containing the word.

Step 2: Look for a definition or for examples of the word in the sentence.

Step 3: Read before or after the sentence for a definition or for examples of the word.

Word Meaning from Context

Lesson 4

Fluency Practice: Information Learned

Name _____ Date _____

The Basics of Bird Flu

Bird flu is an infection caused by a virus. Bird flu is also called avian flu. It occurs naturally in birds, but most wild birds don't become sick from it. It spreads easily to domestic birds. Chickens, turkeys, and geese can become quite ill. In rare cases, humans can catch the disease from infected birds. Millions of birds and several humans have died from bird flu.

How the Virus Spreads

Strains of the bird flu virus are often carried by ducks and other waterbirds. These birds pass the virus to other birds. The virus spreads through saliva, mucus, and airborne particles. The virus can be carried on tractors, cages, and clothing. Outdoor markets full of birds and people are a good place for spreading the disease. People who have contact with sick birds may become infected. One infected person may spread the disease to another person.

Symptoms and Treatments

Bird flu symptoms are like those of the common flu. They are cough, fever, muscle pain, and sore throat. People infected with a weak strain of the virus may have only a mild eye infection. People infected with a powerful strain may develop serious respiratory problems. Lung problems are the most common cause of death in patients.

The Federal Drug Administration has approved four drugs for the treatment of bird flu. However, viruses can change their genetic makeup. They may become resistant to the drugs. Then the drugs will no longer work.

Prevention

There is now a vaccine to protect against the most dangerous strain of bird flu. So far, it seems to be working. However, scientists worry that someday the virus may become immune to this vaccine. The first defense against avian flu is to avoid travel to regions where outbreaks have occurred. Here's what you can do to prevent the spread of the disease. Wash your hands often. Don't eat raw eggs. Be sure the poultry you eat is fully cooked. These steps will help keep you safe.

. . . .

Directions: Write three things you learned from reading the fluency passage.

1. I learned _____

_____

2. I learned _____

_____

3. I learned _____

_____

Think-Pair-Share

Name _____ Date _____

Directions

Directions: Use the think-pair-share strategy to complete the question below.

Step 1: **Think** about the question for one minute.

Step 2: **Pair** and complete the question with your partner.

Step 3: **Share** what you wrote with the class.

Apply

Suppose you're a scientist studying infectious diseases. *Apply* your knowledge of viruses to prove you've discovered a new virus. Develop a name for the new virus.

Lesson
1

Text-Connections Chart

Name _____ Date _____

1

What's the topic of the lesson? _____

_____

_____

2

What's your purpose for reading? _____

_____

_____

3

What do you know about the topic? _____

_____

_____

_____

_____

_____

_____

_____

_____

_____

Order-or-Sequence Chart

Name _____ Date _____

```
┌─────────────────────────────────────────┐
│                                         │
└─────────────────────────────────────────┘
                    ↓
┌─────────────────────────────────────────┐
│                                         │
└─────────────────────────────────────────┘
                    ↓
┌─────────────────────────────────────────┐
│                                         │
└─────────────────────────────────────────┘
                    ↓
┌─────────────────────────────────────────┐
│                                         │
└─────────────────────────────────────────┘
                    ↓
┌─────────────────────────────────────────┐
│                                         │
└─────────────────────────────────────────┘
                    ↓
┌─────────────────────────────────────────┐
│                                         │
└─────────────────────────────────────────┘
                    ↓
┌─────────────────────────────────────────┐
│                                         │
└─────────────────────────────────────────┘
                    ↓
┌─────────────────────────────────────────┐
│                                         │
└─────────────────────────────────────────┘
```

Lesson
1

Context-Clues Strategy

Name _____ Date _____

Decoding-Multipart-Words Strategy

Step 1: Underline all the vowel sounds.

Step 2: Make a slash between the word parts so each part has one vowel sound.

Step 3: Go back to the beginning of the word, and read the parts in order.

Step 4: Read the whole word.

Word

Context-Clues Strategy

When you come across a word you don't know,

Step 1: Read the sentence containing the word.

Step 2: Look for a definition or for examples of the word in the sentence.

Step 3: Read before or after the sentence for a definition or for examples of the word.

Word Meaning from Context

Lesson 2

Text-Connections Chart

Name _____ Date _____

1

What's the topic of the lesson? _____

_____

_____

2

What's your purpose for reading? _____

_____

_____

3

What do you know about the topic? _____

_____

_____

_____

_____

_____

_____

_____

_____

Activity 2

Lesson 2

Cause-and-Effect Chart

Name _____ Date _____

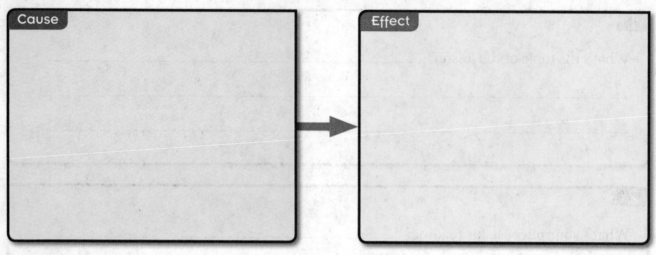

Cause → Effect

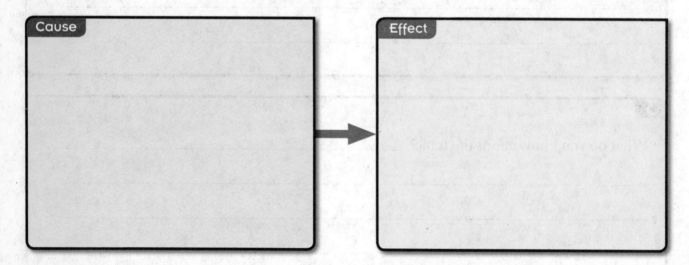

Cause → Effect

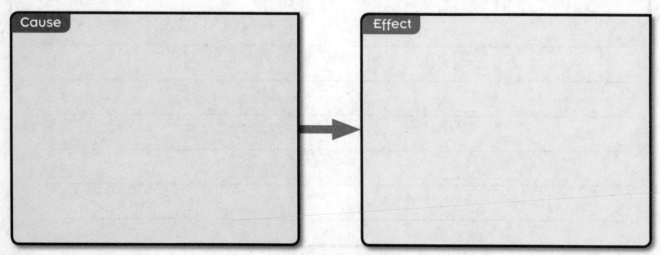

Cause → Effect

Context-Clues Strategy

Name _____ Date _____

Decoding-Multipart-Words Strategy

Step 1: Underline all the vowel sounds.

Step 2: Make a slash between the word parts so each part has one vowel sound.

Step 3: Go back to the beginning of the word, and read the parts in order.

Step 4: Read the whole word.

Word

Context-Clues Strategy

When you come across a word you don't know,

Step 1: Read the sentence containing the word.

Step 2: Look for a definition or for examples of the word in the sentence.

Step 3: Read before or after the sentence for a definition or for examples of the word.

Word Meaning from Context

Fluency Practice: Decoding Multipart Words

Name _____ Date _____

The Female Pharaoh

Almost thirty-five hundred years ago along the Nile River, the pharaoh Thutmose II lived with his queen, Hatshepsut. Hatshepsut was also Thutmose's sister. (Pharaohs often married their sisters in ancient Egypt.) Another wife was the mother of his son Thutmose III. Hatshepsut was little Thutmose's aunt and stepmother.

When the pharaoh died, Thutmose III inherited the throne. The boy was still very young, so Hatshepsut became his regent. She was the person who actually ruled.

After Thutmose grew up, Hatshepsut continued to govern. She even called herself king. Court sculptors made images of her wearing a long, fake beard. The beard symbolized power.

Egypt enjoyed peace and prosperity during Hatshepsut's reign. Royal families before hers had made enemies of Egypt's trading partners. She restored trade with lands to the west, east, and south. The nation's economy boomed.

Art and architecture also flowered under the female pharaoh. She had old monuments repaired and new ones built. She encouraged artists to produce new kinds of art.

After Hatshepsut died, Thutmose ruled Egypt for thirty-three more years. For some reason, Thutmose destroyed the statues of Hatshepsut and erased her name from all monuments. Her memory survived. In 300 B.C., a priest named Manetho mentioned the female pharaoh and her rule of twenty-one years in his history of Egypt.

Hatshepsut's mummy was discovered in Egypt's Valley of the Kings about A.D. 1900. Nobody knew who the mummy was. A clue to the identity was in a box from another tomb uncovered in 1881. On the box was Hatshepsut's name. In the box were mummified organs and a tooth. In 2007, researchers compared the tooth with an empty socket in the unidentified mummy's jaw. The tooth and socket were a perfect fit. Further examination of the mummy showed that Hatshepsut died of bone cancer at age fifty. Her mummy is now on display at Cairo's Egyptian Museum.

• •

Strategy Steps

Step 1: Underline all the vowel sounds.

Step 2: Make a slash between the word parts so each part has one vowel sound.

Step 3: Go back to the beginning of the word, and read the parts in order.

Step 4: Read the whole word.

Word 1

Word 2

Lesson 3

Text-Connections Chart

Name _____ Date _____

1

What's the topic of the lesson? _____

_____

_____

2

What's your purpose for reading? _____

_____

_____

3

What do you know about the topic? _____

_____

_____

_____

_____

_____

_____

_____

_____

Lesson 3

Compare-and-Contrast Chart

Name _____ Date _____

Different	Same	Different

Lesson 3

Context-Clues Strategy

Name _____ Date _____

Decoding-Multipart-Words Strategy

Step 1: Underline all the vowel sounds.

Step 2: Make a slash between the word parts so each part has one vowel sound.

Step 3: Go back to the beginning of the word, and read the parts in order.

Step 4: Read the whole word.

Word

Context-Clues Strategy

When you come across a word you don't know,

Step 1: Read the sentence containing the word.

Step 2: Look for a definition or for examples of the word in the sentence.

Step 3: Read before or after the sentence for a definition or for examples of the word.

Word Meaning from Context

Fluency Practice: Standardized Test

Name _____ Date _____

The Female Pharaoh

Almost thirty-five hundred years ago along the Nile River, the pharaoh Thutmose II lived with his queen, Hatshepsut. Hatshepsut was also Thutmose's sister. (Pharaohs often married their sisters in ancient Egypt.) Another wife was the mother of his son Thutmose III. Hatshepsut was little Thutmose's aunt and stepmother.

When the pharaoh died, Thutmose III inherited the throne. The boy was still very young, so Hatshepsut became his regent. She was the person who actually ruled.

After Thutmose grew up, Hatshepsut continued to govern. She even called herself king. Court sculptors made images of her wearing a long, fake beard. The beard symbolized power.

Egypt enjoyed peace and prosperity during Hatshepsut's reign. Royal families before hers had made enemies of Egypt's trading partners. She restored trade with lands to the west, east, and south. The nation's economy boomed.

Art and architecture also flowered under the female pharaoh. She had old monuments repaired and new ones built. She encouraged artists to produce new kinds of art.

After Hatshepsut died, Thutmose ruled Egypt for thirty-three more years. For some reason, Thutmose destroyed the statues of Hatshepsut and erased her name from all monuments. Her memory survived. In 300 B.C., a priest named Manetho mentioned the female pharaoh and her rule of twenty-one years in his history of Egypt.

Hatshepsut's mummy was discovered in Egypt's Valley of the Kings about A.D. 1900. Nobody knew who the mummy was. A clue to the identity was in a box from another tomb uncovered in 1881. On the box was Hatshepsut's name. In the box were mummified organs and a tooth. In 2007, researchers compared the tooth with an empty socket in the unidentified mummy's jaw. The tooth and socket were a perfect fit. Further examination of the mummy showed that Hatshepsut died of bone cancer at age fifty. Her mummy is now on display at Cairo's Egyptian Museum.

• •

Score _____ /8 = _____ %

Directions: Take turns reading the questions. Answer the questions together.

| Level 1: "Remember" Questions—each worth 1 point |

For Level 1 questions, fill in the space next to the correct answer in your own Workbook.

1. The pharaoh Thutmose II and Queen Hatshepsut lived
   ○ a. almost thirty-five hundred years ago.
   ○ b. almost five thousand years ago.
   ○ c. almost five hundred years ago.
   ○ d. almost fifteen hundred years ago.

Lesson 3

Fluency Practice: Standardized Test, continued

Name _____ Date _____

2. Hatshepsut was Thutmose II's wife and

- ○ a. niece.
- ○ b. cousin.
- ○ c. sister.
- ○ d. aunt.

3. What symbolized a pharaoh's power?

- ○ a. A tall hat
- ○ b. A beard
- ○ c. A long robe
- ○ d. A gold ring

4. What happened to Egypt's economy during Hatshepsut's reign?

- ○ a. The economy suffered.
- ○ b. The economy strengthened.
- ○ c. The economy didn't change.
- ○ d. None of the above

5. What did Thutmose III do after Hatshepsut died?

- ○ a. He put up more monuments and statues in Hatshepsut's name.
- ○ b. He stopped ruling Egypt because of his grief and despair over her death.
- ○ c. He destroyed the statues of Hatshepsut and erased her name from all monuments.
- ○ d. He celebrated Hatshepsut's death.

6. How was Hatshepsut's mummy identified after the tombs were discovered?

- ○ a. The mummy wore a bracelet with Hatshepsut's name engraved on it.
- ○ b. Researchers compared a tooth of Hatshepsut's with an empty socket in an unidentified mummy's jaw.
- ○ c. The tomb was clearly marked with Hatshepsut's name.
- ○ d. DNA testing of a proved the mummy was Hatshepsut.

Level 2: "Understand" Question—worth 2 points (2 points for correct answer, 1 point for partially correct answer, 0 points for incorrect answer)

For the Level 2 question, write the answer in the space provided in your own Workbook.

7. Describe <u>two</u> ways Egypt enjoyed peace and prosperity during Hatshepsut's reign as "king."

_____

_____

_____

_____

Lesson 4

Text-Connections Chart

Name _____ Date _____

1

What's the topic of the lesson? _____

_____

_____

2

What's your purpose for reading? _____

_____

_____

3

What do you know about the topic? _____

_____

_____

_____

_____

_____

_____

_____

_____

_____

_____

Lesson
4

Description-or-List Chart

Name _____ Date _____

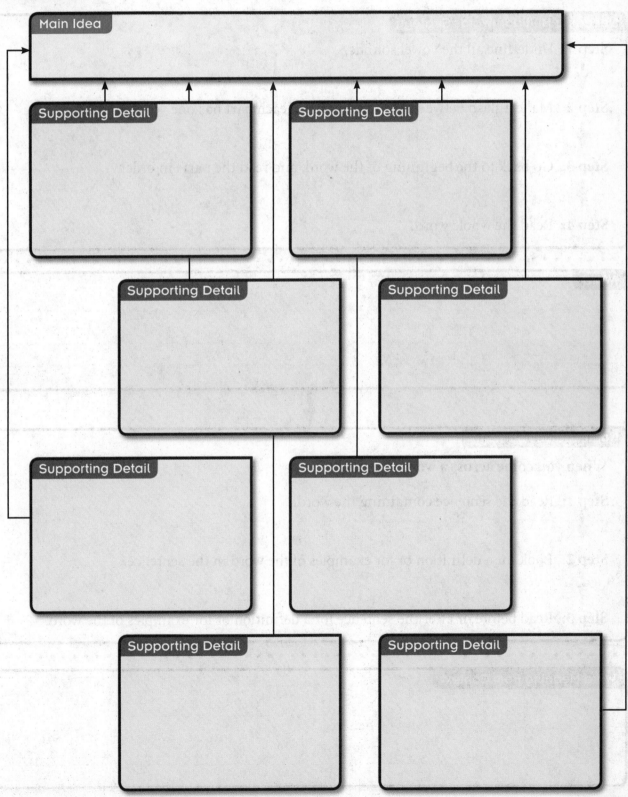

Main Idea

Supporting Detail

Supporting Detail

Supporting Detail

Supporting Detail

Supporting Detail

Supporting Detail

Supporting Detail

Supporting Detail

Context-Clues Strategy

Name _____ Date _____

Decoding-Multipart-Words Strategy

Step 1: Underline all the vowel sounds.

Step 2: Make a slash between the word parts so each part has one vowel sound.

Step 3: Go back to the beginning of the word, and read the parts in order.

Step 4: Read the whole word.

Word

Context-Clues Strategy

When you come across a word you don't know,

Step 1: Read the sentence containing the word.

Step 2: Look for a definition or for examples of the word in the sentence.

Step 3: Read before or after the sentence for a definition or for examples of the word.

Word Meaning from Context

Fluency Practice: Information Learned

Name _____ Date _____

The Female Pharaoh

Almost thirty-five hundred years ago along the Nile River, the pharaoh Thutmose II lived with his queen, Hatshepsut. Hatshepsut was also Thutmose's sister. (Pharaohs often married their sisters in ancient Egypt.) Another wife was the mother of his son Thutmose III. Hatshepsut was little Thutmose's aunt and stepmother.

When the pharaoh died, Thutmose III inherited the throne. The boy was still very young, so Hatshepsut became his regent. She was the person who actually ruled.

After Thutmose grew up, Hatshepsut continued to govern. She even called herself king. Court sculptors made images of her wearing a long, fake beard. The beard symbolized power.

Egypt enjoyed peace and prosperity during Hatshepsut's reign. Royal families before hers had made enemies of Egypt's trading partners. She restored trade with lands to the west, east, and south. The nation's economy boomed.

Art and architecture also flowered under the female pharaoh. She had old monuments repaired and new ones built. She encouraged artists to produce new kinds of art.

After Hatshepsut died, Thutmose ruled Egypt for thirty-three more years. For some reason, Thutmose destroyed the statues of Hatshepsut and erased her name from all monuments. Her memory survived. In 300 B.C., a priest named Manetho mentioned the female pharaoh and her rule of twenty-one years in his history of Egypt.

Hatshepsut's mummy was discovered in Egypt's Valley of the Kings about A.D. 1900. Nobody knew who the mummy was. A clue to the identity was in a box from another tomb uncovered in 1881. On the box was Hatshepsut's name. In the box were mummified organs and a tooth. In 2007, researchers compared the tooth with an empty socket in the unidentified mummy's jaw. The tooth and socket were a perfect fit. Further examination of the mummy showed that Hatshepsut died of bone cancer at age fifty. Her mummy is now on display at Cairo's Egyptian Museum.

• •

Directions: Write three things you learned from reading the fluency passage.

1. I learned _____

_____

2. I learned _____

_____

3. I learned _____

Lesson 5

Think-Pair-Share

Name _____ Date _____

Directions

Directions: Use the Think-Pair-Share Strategy to complete the question below.

Step 1: **Think** about the question for one minute.

Step 2: **Pair** and complete the question with your partner.

Step 3: **Share** what you wrote with the class.

Apply

Suppose you're a news reporter in the Middle Ages who's interviewing a serf. *Apply* your knowledge of feudalism to develop three questions you would ask. Then develop the most likely responses to these questions.

Text-Connections Chart

Name _____ Date _____

1

What's the topic of the lesson? _____

_____

_____

2

What's your purpose for reading? _____

_____

_____

3

What do you know about the topic? _____

_____

_____

_____

_____

_____

_____

_____

_____

Lesson

1

Cause-and-Effect Chart

Name _____ Date _____

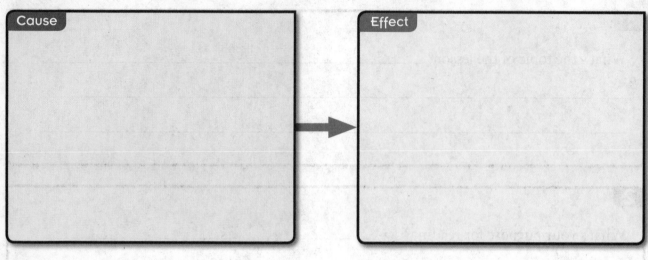

Cause

Effect

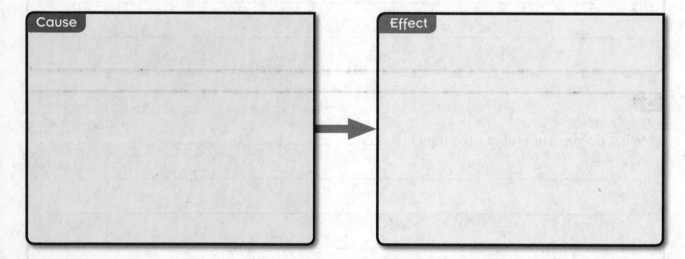

Cause

Effect

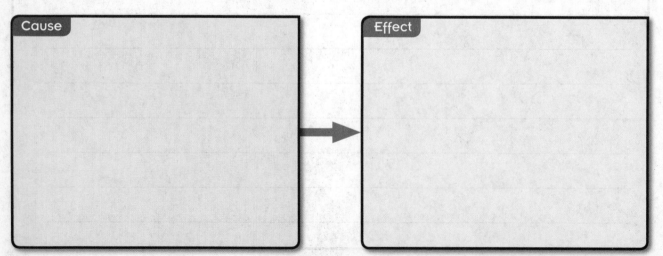

Cause

Effect

Lesson
1

Context-Clues Strategy

Name _____ Date _____

Decoding-Multipart-Words Strategy

Step 1: Underline all the vowel sounds.

Step 2: Make a slash between the word parts so each part has one vowel sound.

Step 3: Go back to the beginning of the word, and read the parts in order.

Step 4: Read the whole word.

Word

Context-Clues Strategy

When you come across a word you don't know,

Step 1: Read the sentence containing the word.

Step 2: Look for a definition or for examples of the word in the sentence.

Step 3: Read before or after the sentence for a definition or for examples of the word.

Word Meaning from Context

Text-Connections Chart

Name _____ Date _____

1

What's the topic of the lesson? _____

_____

_____

2

What's your purpose for reading? _____

_____

_____

3

What do you know about the topic? _____

_____

_____

_____

_____

_____

_____

_____

_____

_____

Lesson
2

Compare-and-Contrast Chart

Name _____ Date _____

Different	Same	Different

Context-Clues Strategy

Name _____ Date _____

Decoding-Multipart-Words Strategy

Step 1: Underline all the vowel sounds.

Step 2: Make a slash between the word parts so each part has one vowel sound.

Step 3: Go back to the beginning of the word, and read the parts in order.

Step 4: Read the whole word.

Word

Context-Clues Strategy

When you come across a word you don't know,

Step 1: Read the sentence containing the word.

Step 2: Look for a definition or for examples of the word in the sentence.

Step 3: Read before or after the sentence for a definition or for examples of the word.

Word Meaning from Context

Fluency Practice: Decoding Multipart Words

Name _____ Date _____

Mansa Musa

Mali lies at the edge of the Sahara. In 1300, Mali's rulers controlled the trade routes across the desert. Caravans carried gold, salt, ivory, kola nuts, and enslaved people along these routes.

In 1312, Mansa Musa became Mali's king. Musa was a devout Muslim. Islam requires its followers to make at least one pilgrimage to Mecca. Mecca is in Saudi Arabia. Musa went to Mecca in 1324 to fulfill his religious obligation. He also had another reason for going. He wanted to impress the world with Mali's wealth.

On the way to Mecca, Musa traveled through Cairo. He led a marvelous caravan into the city. His attendants included sixty thousand people and eighty camels. The camels carried tons of gold that Musa gave to the poor. Musa distributed so much gold that its value fell in Egypt and stayed low for many years.

Musa expanded his empire by seizing nearby lands and Timbuktu. Located where the Niger River meets the desert, Timbuktu had been a trade center for centuries. Merchants from the Arabian Peninsula to the Mediterranean Sea looked to Timbuktu for gold, salt, and books.

Scholars also looked to Timbuktu. They came from all over Africa to Timbuktu's universities and Islamic schools. These institutions not only produced new books but also imported old ones to fill Timbuktu's libraries. In addition, the city had flourishing book-copying businesses. At the time, all books were copied by hand because printing presses did not yet exist.

The emperor brought the famous Egyptian architect Saheli to the city. Musa paid Saheli a small fortune to design the grand Friday Prayers Mosque. For building materials, Saheli used bricks and mud—a first in this region of Africa. For almost seven hundred years, the people of Timbuktu have used mud to replaster the mosque walls each summer.

Timbuktu became Musa's main legacy. It remained Africa's Islamic hub long after the Mali empire fell in the fifteenth century. Muslims of the city still gather at the mosque Musa built.

Strategy Steps

Step 1: Underline all the vowel sounds.

Step 2: Make a slash between the word parts so each part has one vowel sound.

Step 3: Go back to the beginning of the word, and read the parts in order.

Step 4: Read the whole word.

Word 1

Word 2

Lesson 3

Text-Connections Chart

Name _____ Date _____

1

What's the topic of the lesson? _____
_____
_____

2

What's your purpose for reading? _____
_____
_____

3

What do you know about the topic? _____
_____
_____
_____
_____
_____
_____
_____
_____
_____

Lesson 3

Description-or-List Chart

Name _____ Date _____

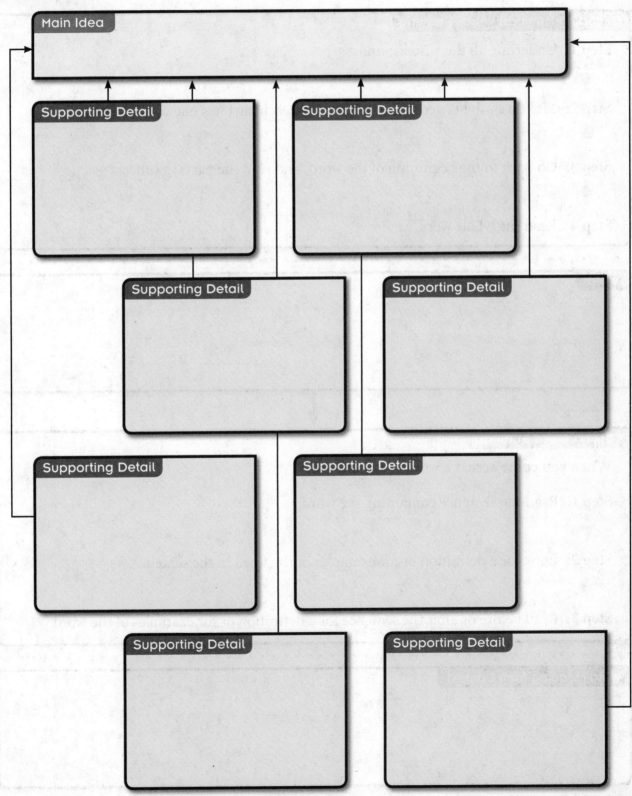

Main Idea

Supporting Detail

Supporting Detail

Supporting Detail

Supporting Detail

Supporting Detail

Supporting Detail

Supporting Detail

Supporting Detail

Lesson
3

Context-Clues Strategy

Name _____ Date _____

Decoding-Multipart-Words Strategy

Step 1: Underline all the vowel sounds.

Step 2: Make a slash between the word parts so each part has one vowel sound.

Step 3: Go back to the beginning of the word, and read the parts in order.

Step 4: Read the whole word.

Word

Context-Clues Strategy

When you come across a word you don't know,

Step 1: Read the sentence containing the word.

Step 2: Look for a definition or for examples of the word in the sentence.

Step 3: Read before or after the sentence for a definition or for examples of the word.

Word Meaning from Context

Lesson 3

Fluency Practice: Standardized Test

Name _____ Date _____

Mansa Musa

Mali lies at the edge of the Sahara. In 1300, Mali's rulers controlled the trade routes across the desert. Caravans carried gold, salt, ivory, kola nuts, and enslaved people along these routes.

In 1312, Mansa Musa became Mali's king. Musa was a devout Muslim. Islam requires its followers to make at least one pilgrimage to Mecca. Mecca is in Saudi Arabia. Musa went to Mecca in 1324 to fulfill his religious obligation. He also had another reason for going. He wanted to impress the world with Mali's wealth.

On the way to Mecca, Musa traveled through Cairo. He led a marvelous caravan into the city. His attendants included sixty thousand people and eighty camels. The camels carried tons of gold that Musa gave to the poor. Musa distributed so much gold that its value fell in Egypt and stayed low for many years.

Musa expanded his empire by seizing nearby lands and Timbuktu. Located where the Niger River meets the desert, Timbuktu had been a trade center for centuries. Merchants from the Arabian Peninsula to the Mediterranean Sea looked to Timbuktu for gold, salt, and books.

Scholars also looked to Timbuktu. They came from all over Africa to Timbuktu's universities and Islamic schools. These institutions not only produced new books but also imported old ones to fill Timbuktu's libraries. In addition, the city had flourishing book-copying businesses. At the time, all books were copied by hand because printing presses did not yet exist.

The emperor brought the famous Egyptian architect Saheli to the city. Musa paid Saheli a small fortune to design the grand Friday Prayers Mosque. For building materials, Saheli used bricks and mud—a first in this region of Africa. For almost seven hundred years, the people of Timbuktu have used mud to replaster the mosque walls each summer.

Timbuktu became Musa's main legacy. It remained Africa's Islamic hub long after the Mali empire fell in the fifteenth century. Muslims of the city still gather at the mosque Musa built.

· ·

Score _____ /8 = _____ %

Directions: Take turns reading the questions. Answer the questions together.

| **Level 1:** "Remember" Questions—each worth 1 point |

For Level 1 questions, fill in the space next to the correct answer in your own Workbook.

1. Mali's rulers controlled trade routes that helped transport
   ○ a. silver and cattle.　　○ c. machines.
   ○ b. oil.　　　　　　　　○ d. gold and ivory.

Lesson 3

Fluency Practice: Standardized Test, continued

Name _____ Date _____

2. Islam requires its followers to
   ○ a. make at least one pilgrimage to Mecca.
   ○ b. live in Saudi Arabia near Mecca.
   ○ c. attend university in Timbuktu.
   ○ d. marry by the age of eighteen.

3. What happened when Musa traveled through Cairo on his way to Mecca?
   ○ a. Most of Musa's caravan died from disease and exhaustion.
   ○ b. Musa gave away so much gold its value fell.
   ○ c. Musa considered declaring war on Saudi Arabia.
   ○ d. Musa liked Cairo and its people so much he never left.

4. How did Musa expand his empire?
   ○ a. He seized nearby lands.   ○ c. He seized the Arabian Peninsula.
   ○ b. He took control of the Niger River.   ○ d. He purchased large areas of land.

5. How were books copied in Timbuktu during Musa's reign?
   ○ a. By computer
   ○ b. By printing press
   ○ c. By hand
   ○ d. Books weren't copied.

6. What became Musa's main legacy?
   ○ a. The use of the printing press
   ○ b. The use of bricks and mud as building materials
   ○ c. The city of Timbuktu
   ○ d. The hiring of the famous Egyptian architect Saheli

Level 2: "Understand" Question—worth 2 points (2 points for correct answer, 1 point for partially correct answer, 0 points for incorrect answer)

For the Level 2 question, write the answer in the space provided in your own Workbook.

7. Explain what Saheli used to build the grand Friday Prayers Mosque and why this was an important decision in Timbuktu's history.

   _____

   _____

   _____

Text-Connections Chart

Name _____ Date _____

1

What's the topic of the lesson? _____

_____

_____

2

What's your purpose for reading? _____

_____

_____

3

What do you know about the topic? _____

_____

_____

_____

_____

_____

_____

_____

_____

Lesson 4

Order-or-Sequence Chart

Name _____ Date _____

Lesson 4

Context-Clues Strategy

Name _____ Date _____

Decoding-Multipart-Words-Strategy

Step 1: Underline all the vowel sounds.

Step 2: Make a slash between the word parts so each part has one vowel sound.

Step 3: Go back to the beginning of the word, and read the parts in order.

Step 4: Read the whole word.

Word

Context-Clues Strategy

When you come across a word you don't know,

Step 1: Read the sentence containing the word.

Step 2: Look for a definition or for examples of the word in the sentence.

Step 3: Read before or after the sentence for a definition or for examples of the word.

Word Meaning from Context

Fluency Practice: Information Learned

Name _____ Date _____

Mansa Musa

Mali lies at the edge of the Sahara. In 1300, Mali's rulers controlled the trade routes across the desert. Caravans carried gold, salt, ivory, kola nuts, and enslaved people along these routes.

In 1312, Mansa Musa became Mali's king. Musa was a devout Muslim. Islam requires its followers to make at least one pilgrimage to Mecca. Mecca is in Saudi Arabia. Musa went to Mecca in 1324 to fulfill his religious obligation. He also had another reason for going. He wanted to impress the world with Mali's wealth.

On the way to Mecca, Musa traveled through Cairo. He led a marvelous caravan into the city. His attendants included sixty thousand people and eighty camels. The camels carried tons of gold that Musa gave to the poor. Musa distributed so much gold that its value fell in Egypt and stayed low for many years.

Musa expanded his empire by seizing nearby lands and Timbuktu. Located where the Niger River meets the desert, Timbuktu had been a trade center for centuries. Merchants from the Arabian Peninsula to the Mediterranean Sea looked to Timbuktu for gold, salt, and books.

Scholars also looked to Timbuktu. They came from all over Africa to Timbuktu's universities and Islamic schools. These institutions not only produced new books but also imported old ones to fill Timbuktu's libraries. In addition, the city had flourishing book-copying businesses. At the time, all books were copied by hand because printing presses did not yet exist.

The emperor brought the famous Egyptian architect Saheli to the city. Musa paid Saheli a small fortune to design the grand Friday Prayers Mosque. For building materials, Saheli used bricks and mud—a first in this region of Africa. For almost seven hundred years, the people of Timbuktu have used mud to replaster the mosque walls each summer.

Timbuktu became Musa's main legacy. It remained Africa's Islamic hub long after the Mali empire fell in the fifteenth century. Muslims of the city still gather at the mosque Musa built.

Directions: Write three things you learned from reading the fluency passage.

1. I learned _____

_____

2. I learned _____

_____

3. I learned _____

_____

Lesson
5

Think-Pair-Share

Name _____ Date _____

Directions: Use the Think-Pair-Share Strategy to complete the question below.

Step 1: **Think** about the question for one minute.

Step 2: **Pair** and complete the question with your partner.

Step 3: **Share** what you wrote with the class.

Apply

Suppose you're preparing a speech about why you're proud of the United States. *Apply* your knowledge of nationalism to develop three statements you will include in your speech.

Lesson 1

Text-Connections Chart

Name _____ Date _____

1

What's the topic of the lesson? _____

_____

_____

2

What's your purpose for reading? _____

_____

_____

3

What do you know about the topic? _____

_____

_____

_____

_____

_____

_____

_____

_____

Lesson 1

Compare-and-Contrast Chart

Name _____ Date _____

Different	Same	Different

Lesson 1

Context-Clues Strategy

Name _____ Date_____

Decoding-Multipart-Words Strategy

Step 1: Underline all the vowel sounds.

Step 2: Make a slash between the word parts so each part has one vowel sound.

Step 3: Go back to the beginning of the word, and read the parts in order.

Step 4: Read the whole word.

Word

Context-Clues Strategy

When you come across a word you don't know,

Step 1: Read the sentence containing the word.

Step 2: Look for a definition or for examples of the word in the sentence.

Step 3: Read before or after the sentence for a definition or for examples of the word.

Word Meaning from Context

Lesson 2

Description-or-List Chart

Name _____ Date _____

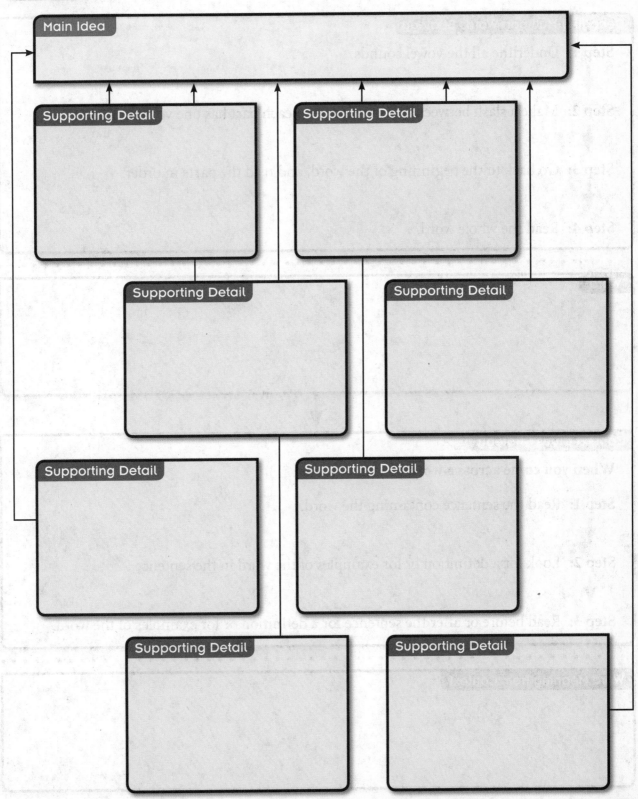

Main Idea

Supporting Detail

Supporting Detail

Supporting Detail

Supporting Detail

Supporting Detail

Supporting Detail

Supporting Detail

Supporting Detail

Lesson 2

Context-Clues Strategy

Name _____ Date _____

Decoding-Multipart-Words Strategy

Step 1: Underline all the vowel sounds.

Step 2: Make a slash between the word parts so each part has one vowel sound.

Step 3: Go back to the beginning of the word, and read the parts in order.

Step 4: Read the whole word.

Word

Context-Clues Strategy

When you come across a word you don't know,

Step 1: Read the sentence containing the word.

Step 2: Look for a definition or for examples of the word in the sentence.

Step 3: Read before or after the sentence for a definition or for examples of the word.

Word Meaning from Context

Lesson
2

Fluency Practice: Decoding Multipart Words

Name _____ Date _____

Attack of the Flesh-Eating Bacteria

When Bacteria Turn Bad

There are many types of bacteria in our bodies. Some bacteria are helpful. Others are harmful. In rare cases, bacteria spread fast and can be deadly. One form of these invasive infections is known as flesh-eating bacteria.

The bacteria that cause these infections are common. Chances are you have at one time been infected with them. They cause strep throat and impetigo, a skin infection. Luckily, most of these infections are mild. In fact, some people carry these bacteria in their bodies without getting sick at all. Under certain conditions, they can cause serious, life-threatening infections.

Trouble occurs when bacteria invade the body through sores or cuts. Despite their name, flesh-eating bacteria don't actually eat flesh. They release toxins when they invade skin, muscle, or other tissues and destroy the tissue. The infection causes tissue damage because it spreads quickly.

Treatment

The key to surviving an attack of flesh-eating bacteria is to seek medical help right away. Patients receive powerful antibiotic drugs to fight the infection. Surgery may be necessary to remove tissue damaged by toxins. Unfortunately, large amounts of tissue must sometimes be removed. In severe cases, there is so much tissue damage that patients must have body parts amputated, or cut off. Most patients are left with scars as a result of the damage caused by the infection. About 25 percent of patients infected with flesh-eating bacteria do not survive, even after they have received medical care.

Hope and Prevention

Fortunately, cases of flesh-eating bacteria are rare. Each year there are about ten million cases of infections caused by strep bacteria. Only about five hundred of these patients develop a flesh-eating infection.

Bacterial infections can often be prevented by washing your hands after you cough, sneeze, or prepare food. Keep cuts and sores clean. Follow directions carefully when taking an antibiotic.

Strategy Steps

Step 1: Underline all the vowel sounds.

Step 2: Make a slash between the word parts so each part has one vowel sound.

Step 3: Go back to the beginning of the word, and read the parts in order.

Step 4: Read the whole word.

Word 1

Word 2

Lesson 3

Order-or-Sequence Chart

Name _____ Date _____

```
┌─────────────────────────────────────────┐
│                                          │
└─────────────────────────────────────────┘
                    ↓
┌─────────────────────────────────────────┐
│                                          │
└─────────────────────────────────────────┘
                    ↓
┌─────────────────────────────────────────┐
│                                          │
└─────────────────────────────────────────┘
                    ↓
┌─────────────────────────────────────────┐
│                                          │
└─────────────────────────────────────────┘
                    ↓
┌─────────────────────────────────────────┐
│                                          │
└─────────────────────────────────────────┘
                    ↓
┌─────────────────────────────────────────┐
│                                          │
└─────────────────────────────────────────┘
                    ↓
┌─────────────────────────────────────────┐
│                                          │
└─────────────────────────────────────────┘
                    ↓
┌─────────────────────────────────────────┐
│                                          │
└─────────────────────────────────────────┘
```

Lesson 3

Context-Clues Strategy

Name _____ Date _____

Decoding-Multipart-Words Strategy

Step 1: Underline all the vowel sounds.

Step 2: Make a slash between the word parts so each part has one vowel sound.

Step 3: Go back to the beginning of the word, and read the parts in order.

Step 4: Read the whole word.

Word

Context-Clues Strategy

When you come across a word you don't know,

Step 1: Read the sentence containing the word.

Step 2: Look for a definition or for examples of the word in the sentence.

Step 3: Read before or after the sentence for a definition or for examples of the word.

Word Meaning from Context

Lesson 3

Fluency Practice: Standardized Test

Name _____ Date _____

Attack of the Flesh-Eating Bacteria

When Bacteria Turn Bad

There are many types of bacteria in our bodies. Some bacteria are helpful. Others are harmful. In rare cases, bacteria spread fast and can be deadly. One form of these invasive infections is known as flesh-eating bacteria.

The bacteria that cause these infections are common. Chances are you have at one time been infected with them. They cause strep throat and impetigo, a skin infection. Luckily, most of these infections are mild. In fact, some people carry these bacteria in their bodies without getting sick at all. Under certain conditions, they can cause serious, life-threatening infections.

Trouble occurs when bacteria invade the body through sores or cuts. Despite their name, flesh-eating bacteria don't actually eat flesh. They release toxins when they invade skin, muscle, or other tissues and destroy the tissue. The infection causes tissue damage because it spreads quickly.

Treatment

The key to surviving an attack of flesh-eating bacteria is to seek medical help right away. Patients receive powerful antibiotic drugs to fight the infection. Surgery may be necessary to remove tissue damaged by toxins. Unfortunately, large amounts of tissue must sometimes be removed. In severe cases, there is so much tissue damage that patients must have body parts amputated, or cut off. Most patients are left with scars as a result of the damage caused by the infection. About 25 percent of patients infected with flesh-eating bacteria do not survive, even after they have received medical care.

Hope and Prevention

Fortunately, cases of flesh-eating bacteria are rare. Each year there are about ten million cases of infections caused by strep bacteria. Only about five hundred of these patients develop a flesh-eating infection.

Bacterial infections can often be prevented by washing your hands after you cough, sneeze, or prepare food. Keep cuts and sores clean. Follow directions carefully when taking an antibiotic.

Score _____ /8 = _____ %

Directions: Take turns reading the questions. Answer the questions together.

Level 1: "Remember" Questions—each worth 1 point

For Level 1 questions, fill in the space next to the correct answer in your own Workbook.

1. The bacteria that can cause flesh-eating infections are
   - ○ a. rare.
   - ○ c. helpful.
   - ○ b. common.
   - ○ d. new.

Fluency Practice: Standardized Test, continued

Name _____ Date _____

2. The bacteria that can cause flesh-eating infections can also cause impetigo and
   ○ a. strep throat.   ○ c. chicken pox.
   ○ b. blurred vision.   ○ d. measles.

3. How do flesh-eating bacteria destroy the tissue they invade?
   ○ a. They eat away and destroy the tissue.
   ○ b. They release toxins that destroy the tissue.
   ○ c. They make you at risk to more harmful flesh-eating bacteria that spread quickly.
   ○ d. They trigger the body's immune system to attack tissue where the bacteria invaded.

4. What are patients given to fight off flesh-eating bacteria?
   ○ a. An order of bed rest for two weeks
   ○ b. A flesh-eating-bacteria vaccine
   ○ c. Nothing because the bacteria cures itself over time
   ○ d. Powerful antibiotic drugs

5. What percentage of patients infected with flesh-eating bacteria do not survive, even after they've received medical treatment?
   ○ a. 15%
   ○ b. 45%
   ○ c. 25%
   ○ d. 50%

6. The spread of deadly bacterial infections can be prevented by
   ○ a. keeping cuts and sores clean.
   ○ b. taking medicine once a day.
   ○ c. washing your hands once a day.
   ○ d. drinking orange juice every day.

> **Level 2:** "Understand" Question—worth 2 points (2 points for correct answer, 1 point for partially correct answer, 0 points for incorrect answer)

For the Level 2 question, write the answer in the space provided in your own Workbook.

7. Explain how a simple infection can turn into a dangerous, flesh-eating infection.

_____

_____

_____

Lesson 4

Cause-and-Effect Chart

Name _____ Date _____

Cause		Effect
	→	

Cause		Effect
	→	

Cause		Effect
	→	

Lesson 4

Context-Clues Strategy

Name _____ Date _____

Decoding-Multipart-Words Strategy

Step 1: Underline all the vowel sounds.

Step 2: Make a slash between the word parts so each part has one vowel sound.

Step 3: Go back to the beginning of the word, and read the parts in order.

Step 4: Read the whole word.

Word

Context-Clues Strategy

When you come across a word you don't know,

Step 1: Read the sentence containing the word.

Step 2: Look for a definition or for examples of the word in the sentence.

Step 3: Read before or after the sentence for a definition or for examples of the word.

Word Meaning from Context

Lesson 4

Fluency Practice: Information Learned

Name _____ Date _____

Attack of the Flesh-Eating Bacteria

When Bacteria Turn Bad

There are many types of bacteria in our bodies. Some bacteria are helpful. Others are harmful. In rare cases, bacteria spread fast and can be deadly. One form of these invasive infections is known as flesh-eating bacteria.

The bacteria that cause these infections are common. Chances are you have at one time been infected with them. They cause strep throat and impetigo, a skin infection. Luckily, most of these infections are mild. In fact, some people carry these bacteria in their bodies without getting sick at all. Under certain conditions, they can cause serious, life-threatening infections.

Trouble occurs when bacteria invade the body through sores or cuts. Despite their name, flesh-eating bacteria don't actually eat flesh. They release toxins when they invade skin, muscle, or other tissues and destroy the tissue. The infection causes tissue damage because it spreads quickly.

Treatment

The key to surviving an attack of flesh-eating bacteria is to seek medical help right away. Patients receive powerful antibiotic drugs to fight the infection. Surgery may be necessary to remove tissue damaged by toxins. Unfortunately, large amounts of tissue must sometimes be removed. In severe cases, there is so much tissue damage that patients must have body parts amputated, or cut off. Most patients are left with scars as a result of the damage caused by the infection. About 25 percent of patients infected with flesh-eating bacteria do not survive, even after they have received medical care.

Hope and Prevention

Fortunately, cases of flesh-eating bacteria are rare. Each year there are about ten million cases of infections caused by strep bacteria. Only about five hundred of these patients develop a flesh-eating infection.

Bacterial infections can often be prevented by washing your hands after you cough, sneeze, or prepare food. Keep cuts and sores clean. Follow directions carefully when taking an antibiotic.

Directions: Write three things you learned from reading the fluency passage.

1. I learned _____

_____

2. I learned _____

_____

3. I learned _____

_____

Lesson 5

Think-Pair-Share

Name _____ Date _____

Directions

Directions: Use the Think-Pair-Share Strategy to complete the question below.

Step 1: Think about the question for one minute.

Step 2: Pair and complete the question with your partner.

Step 3: Share what you wrote with the class.

Apply

Suppose parts of our planet are no longer able to support plant life. *Apply* your knowledge of the characteristics and growth of plants to develop an artificial environment under a giant dome. Then tell about the important features that will allow your new environment to support plant life.

Lesson

1

Text-Connections Chart

Name _____ Date _____

1

What's the topic of the lesson? _____

_____

_____

2

What's your purpose for reading? _____

_____

_____

3

What do you know about the topic? _____

_____

_____

_____

_____

_____

_____

_____

_____

_____

Lesson
1

Description-or-List Chart

Name _____ Date _____

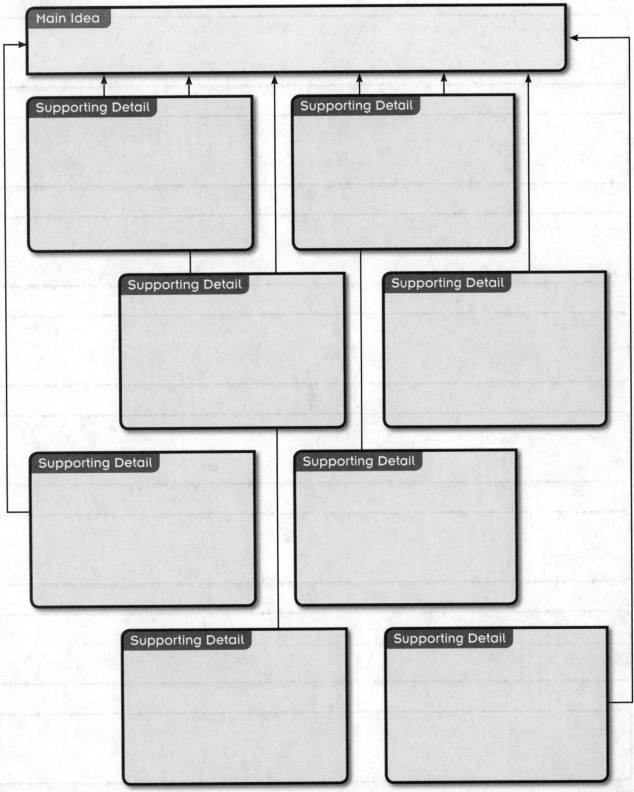

Main Idea

Supporting Detail

Supporting Detail

Supporting Detail

Supporting Detail

Supporting Detail

Supporting Detail

Supporting Detail

Supporting Detail

Lesson
2

Order-or-Sequence Chart

Name _____ Date _____

```
┌─────────────────────────────────────────────────────────┐
│                                                           │
└─────────────────────────────────────────────────────────┘
                            ↓
┌─────────────────────────────────────────────────────────┐
│                                                           │
└─────────────────────────────────────────────────────────┘
                            ↓
┌─────────────────────────────────────────────────────────┐
│                                                           │
└─────────────────────────────────────────────────────────┘
                            ↓
┌─────────────────────────────────────────────────────────┐
│                                                           │
└─────────────────────────────────────────────────────────┘
                            ↓
┌─────────────────────────────────────────────────────────┐
│                                                           │
└─────────────────────────────────────────────────────────┘
                            ↓
┌─────────────────────────────────────────────────────────┐
│                                                           │
└─────────────────────────────────────────────────────────┘
                            ↓
┌─────────────────────────────────────────────────────────┐
│                                                           │
└─────────────────────────────────────────────────────────┘
                            ↓
┌─────────────────────────────────────────────────────────┐
│                                                           │
└─────────────────────────────────────────────────────────┘
```

Lesson 2

Word-Learning Strategies

Name _____ Date _____

Word

Context-Clues Strategy

When you come across a word you don't know,

Step 1: Read the sentence containing the word.

Step 2: Look for a definition or for examples of the word in the sentence.

Step 3: Read before or after the sentence for a definition or for examples of the word.

Word Meaning from Context

Glossary Definition

Dictionary Definition

Online-Dictionary Definition

Fluency Practice: Decoding Multipart Words

Name _____ Date _____

Small Spider, Big Bite

We encounter spiders every day—whether we see them or not. Spiders live outdoors and indoors and in almost every climate on Earth. Most of the time spiders stay hidden from view away from human activity. Have you ever been bitten by a spider? If so, the spider probably injected you with venom. Most spiders aren't as friendly as the one in *Charlotte's Web*. Nearly all of the forty thousand species of spiders are venomous.

Spider Venom

Spiders are predators. Some hunt their prey, and some wait to catch prey in their webs. Venomous spiders inject poison to kill their prey. The venom breaks down the contents of the prey's body and turns it to liquid. The spider uses its mouth parts to suck up the liquid.

Most spiders bite only if they are threatened, trapped, or attacking prey. Although spider venom is designed to kill insects and other tiny prey, organisms as large as humans can have a terrible reaction to the bite of certain spiders.

The Shy Brown Recluse

The brown recluse is a small, shy spider. Its name refers to both its color and its habits. The brown recluse prefers to live in quiet, out-of-the-way places. People sometimes find them in undisturbed places, such as a dark corner in a basement or a box that hasn't been opened for a long time. They also live in barns and garages and under woodpiles.

The brown recluse bites only when it has been disturbed or touched. People can be bitten when they surprise the little brown spider in its hiding place. The bite itself feels like a pinprick. Some people don't even notice it. The spider's venom is poisonous to humans. The victim may experience fever, chills, vomiting, and shock. The venom destroys tissue, forming a hardened crater at the site of the bite. The sore may take weeks or even months to heal completely. Victims are left with a scar as a reminder of their meeting with this spider.

. . . .

Strategy Steps

Step 1: Underline all the vowel sounds.

Step 2: Make a slash between the word parts so each part has one vowel sound.

Step 3: Go back to the beginning of the word, and read the parts in order.

Step 4: Read the whole word.

Word 1

Word 2

Lesson 3

Cause-and-Effect Chart

Name _____ Date _____

Cause		Effect
	→	

Cause		Effect
	→	

Cause		Effect
	→	

Lesson 3

Word-Learning Strategies

Name _____ Date _____

Word

. . . .

Context-Clues Strategy

When you come across a word you don't know,

Step 1: Read the sentence containing the word.

Step 2: Look for a definition or for examples of the word in the sentence.

Step 3: Read before or after the sentence for a definition or for examples of the word.

Word Meaning from Context

Glossary Definition

Dictionary Definition

Online-Dictionary Definition

Lesson 3

Fluency Practice: Standardized Test

Name _____ Date _____

Small Spider, Big Bite

We encounter spiders every day—whether we see them or not. Spiders live outdoors and indoors and in almost every climate on Earth. Most of the time spiders stay hidden from view away from human activity. Have you ever been bitten by a spider? If so, the spider probably injected you with venom. Most spiders aren't as friendly as the one in *Charlotte's Web*. Nearly all of the forty thousand species of spiders are venomous.

Spider Venom

Spiders are predators. Some hunt their prey, and some wait to catch prey in their webs. Venomous spiders inject poison to kill their prey. The venom breaks down the contents of the prey's body and turns it to liquid. The spider uses its mouth parts to suck up the liquid.

Most spiders bite only if they are threatened, trapped, or attacking prey. Although spider venom is designed to kill insects and other tiny prey, organisms as large as humans can have a terrible reaction to the bite of certain spiders.

The Shy Brown Recluse

The brown recluse is a small, shy spider. Its name refers to both its color and its habits. The brown recluse prefers to live in quiet, out-of-the-way places. People sometimes find them in undisturbed places, such as a dark corner in a basement or a box that hasn't been opened for a long time. They also live in barns and garages and under woodpiles.

The brown recluse bites only when it has been disturbed or touched. People can be bitten when they surprise the little brown spider in its hiding place. The bite itself feels like a pinprick. Some people don't even notice it. The spider's venom is poisonous to humans. The victim may experience fever, chills, vomiting, and shock. The venom destroys tissue, forming a hardened crater at the site of the bite. The sore may take weeks or even months to heal completely. Victims are left with a scar as a reminder of their meeting with this spider.

· ·

Score _____ /8 = _____ %

Directions: Take turns reading the questions. Answer the questions together.

Level 1: "Remember" Questions—each worth 1 point

For Level 1 questions, fill in the space next to the correct answer in your own Workbook.

1. What do venomous spiders inject into their prey to kill it?
   - ○ a. Webs
   - ○ b. Saliva
   - ○ c. Poison
   - ○ d. Water

Unit 6
Science

Activity 3

Lesson
3

Fluency Practice: Standardized Test, continued

Name _____ Date _____

2. What does the venom do after it has been injected into the prey's body?
   - ○ a. Breaks down the contents of the prey's body and turns them to liquid
   - ○ b. Makes the prey move uncontrollably
   - ○ c. Turns the prey's liquids into a solid that eventually will be eaten
   - ○ d. Makes the prey blind

3. Which type of prey is spider venom designed to kill?
   - ○ a. Humans
   - ○ b. Large animals such as horses or cows
   - ○ c. Insects and other tiny prey
   - ○ d. Sick and weak animals

4. Where does the brown recluse prefer to live?
   - ○ a. Inside houses in bright and sunny rooms
   - ○ b. In quiet, out-of-the-way places
   - ○ c. In places where there is a great deal of activity
   - ○ d. In cold, damp places with standing water

5. When does the brown recluse bite humans?
   - ○ a. If you walk near its web and the spider senses you
   - ○ b. When prey the spider prefers to eat are nearby and threatened
   - ○ c. When the spider has been disturbed or touched
   - ○ d. When you make a loud noise and scare the spider

6. How long does it take for a brown recluse bite to heal?
   - ○ a. A few hours
   - ○ b. A few days
   - ○ c. A week
   - ○ d. Several weeks

Level 2: "Understand" Question—worth 2 points (2 points for correct answer, 1 point for partially correct answer, 0 points for incorrect answer)

For the Level 2 question, write the answer in the space provided in your own Workbook.

7. Explain how someone could surprise a brown recluse spider and get bitten.

_____

_____

_____

_____

Lesson 4

Compare-and-Contrast Chart

Name _____ Date _____

Different	Same	Different

Lesson
4

Word-Learning Strategies

Name _____ Date _____

Word

....

Context-Clues Strategy

When you come across a word you don't know,

Step 1: Read the sentence containing the word.

Step 2: Look for a definition or for examples of the word in the sentence.

Step 3: Read before or after the sentence for a definition or for examples of the word.

Word Meaning from Context

Glossary Definition

Dictionary Definition

Online-Dictionary Definition

Lesson 4

Fluency Practice: Information Learned

Name _____ Date _____

Small Spider, Big Bite

We encounter spiders every day—whether we see them or not. Spiders live outdoors and indoors and in almost every climate on Earth. Most of the time spiders stay hidden from view away from human activity. Have you ever been bitten by a spider? If so, the spider probably injected you with venom. Most spiders aren't as friendly as the one in *Charlotte's Web*. Nearly all of the forty thousand species of spiders are venomous.

Spider Venom

Spiders are predators. Some hunt their prey, and some wait to catch prey in their webs. Venomous spiders inject poison to kill their prey. The venom breaks down the contents of the prey's body and turns it to liquid. The spider uses its mouth parts to suck up the liquid.

Most spiders bite only if they are threatened, trapped, or attacking prey. Although spider venom is designed to kill insects and other tiny prey, organisms as large as humans can have a terrible reaction to the bite of certain spiders.

The Shy Brown Recluse

The brown recluse is a small, shy spider. Its name refers to both its color and its habits. The brown recluse prefers to live in quiet, out-of-the-way places. People sometimes find them in undisturbed places, such as a dark corner in a basement or a box that hasn't been opened for a long time. They also live in barns and garages and under woodpiles.

The brown recluse bites only when it has been disturbed or touched. People can be bitten when they surprise the little brown spider in its hiding place. The bite itself feels like a pinprick. Some people don't even notice it. The spider's venom is poisonous to humans. The victim may experience fever, chills, vomiting, and shock. The venom destroys tissue, forming a hardened crater at the site of the bite. The sore may take weeks or even months to heal completely. Victims are left with a scar as a reminder of their meeting with this spider.

· ·

Directions: Write three things you learned from reading the fluency passage.

1. I learned _____

_____

2. I learned _____

_____

3. I learned _____

_____

Lesson
5

Think-Pair-Share

Name _____ Date _____

Directions: Use the Think-Pair-Share Strategy to complete the question below.

Step 1: **Think** about the question for one minute.

Step 2: **Pair** and complete the question with your partner.

Step 3: **Share** what you wrote with the class.

Analyze

Suppose you're a scientist studying plant and animal life during the winter months in the Arctic tundra (average temperature –30°F). Use your knowledge of mammalian traits to *analyze* which traits will help you survive and which traits will make it difficult for you to survive.

Lesson
1

Text-Connections Chart

Name _____ Date _____

1

What's the topic of the lesson? _____

_____

_____

2

What's your purpose for reading? _____

_____

_____

3

What do you know about the topic? _____

_____

_____

_____

_____

_____

_____

_____

_____

Order-or-Sequence Chart

Name _____ Date _____

Lesson 1

Word-Learning Strategies

Name _____ Date _____

Word

· ·

Context-Clues Strategy

When you come across a word you don't know,

Step 1: Read the sentence containing the word.

Step 2: Look for a definition or for examples of the word in the sentence.

Step 3: Read before or after the sentence for a definition for or for examples of the word.

Word Meaning from Context

Glossary Definition

Dictionary Definition

Online-Dictionary Definition

Cause-and-Effect Chart

Name _____ Date _____

Cause		Effect

Cause		Effect

Cause		Effect

Word-Learning Strategies

Name _____ Date _____

Word

Context-Clues Strategy

When you come across a word you don't know,

Step 1: Read the sentence containing the word.

Step 2: Look for a definition or for examples of the word in the sentence.

Step 3: Read before or after the sentence for a definition for or for examples of the word.

Word Meaning from Context

Glossary Definition

Dictionary Definition

Online-Dictionary Definition

Lesson 2

Fluency Practice: Decoding Multipart Words

Name _____ Date _____

Defenders of Earth's Ecosystems

Human Impact

Humans, like all living things, depend on the environment for survival. We need soil to grow food, water to drink, and air to breathe. We need other resources to provide shelter. We use resources for fuel to provide electricity and heat for our homes. We use resources to power cars and other vehicles.

Human activity plays a big role in Earth's ecosystems. Cutting down forests and burning fossil fuels are just two things that can change ecosystems. These changes can affect habitats, climate, and food webs in an ecosystem. Many species are unable to survive these changes.

Greenpeace Takes Action

People began to notice the bad effects humans have on ecosystems. Groups formed to raise public awareness about these problems. In 1971, Greenpeace was founded to draw attention to issues that affect Earth's ecosystems. Today, millions of people around the world assist Greenpeace.

Forests

Greenpeace supports efforts to protect forests around the world. Forests are home to more organisms than any other type of ecosystem. Forests provide oxygen and lumber. Tree roots prevent soil from washing away.

Greenpeace works to protect forests by encouraging forest-friendly practices and speaking out against activities that harm forests. Greenpeace works to stop logging practices that destroy ancient forests. It also supports the replanting of forests. Greenpeace promotes the harvesting of forest products that don't require cutting down trees. These products include fruits, nuts, rubber, and medicinal extracts.

The Future

Human activities threaten many of Earth's ecosystems, but it is possible to slow this process. Greenpeace urges people to limit their use of natural resources. Using less energy may slow climate change.

Strategy Steps

Step 1: Underline all the vowel sounds.

Step 2: Make a slash between the word parts so each part has one vowel sound.

Step 3: Go back to the beginning of the word, and read the parts in order.

Step 4: Read the whole word.

Word 1

Word 2

Compare-and-Contrast Chart

Name _____ Date _____

Different	Same	Different

Word-Learning Strategies

Name _____ Date _____

Word

· ·

Context-Clues Strategy

When you come across a word you don't know,

Step 1: Read the sentence containing the word.

Step 2: Look for a definition or for examples of the word in the sentence.

Step 3: Read before or after the sentence for a definition for or for examples of the word.

Word Meaning from Context

Glossary Definition

Dictionary Definition

Online-Dictionary Definition

Lesson 3

Fluency Practice: Standardized Test
Defenders of Earth's Ecosystems

Name _____ Date _____

Human Impact

Humans, like all living things, depend on the environment for survival. We need soil to grow food, water to drink, and air to breathe. We need other resources to provide shelter. We use resources for fuel to provide electricity and heat for our homes. We use resources to power cars and other vehicles.

Human activity plays a big role in Earth's ecosystems. Cutting down forests and burning fossil fuels are just two things that can change ecosystems. These changes can affect habitats, climate, and food webs in an ecosystem. Many species are unable to survive these changes.

Greenpeace Takes Action

People began to notice the bad effects humans have on ecosystems. Groups formed to raise public awareness about these problems. In 1971, Greenpeace was founded to draw attention to issues that affect Earth's ecosystems. Today, millions of people around the world assist Greenpeace.

Forests

Greenpeace supports efforts to protect forests around the world. Forests are home to more organisms than any other type of ecosystem. Forests provide oxygen and lumber. Tree roots prevent soil from washing away.

Greenpeace works to protect forests by encouraging forest-friendly practices and speaking out against activities that harm forests. Greenpeace works to stop logging practices that destroy ancient forests. It also supports the replanting of forests. Greenpeace promotes the harvesting of forest products that don't require cutting down trees. These products include fruits, nuts, rubber, and medicinal extracts.

The Future

Human activities threaten many of Earth's ecosystems, but it is possible to slow this process. Greenpeace urges people to limit their use of natural resources. Using less energy may slow climate change.

· ·

Score _____ /8 = _____ %

Directions: Take turns reading the questions. Answer the questions together.

Level 1: "Remember" Questions—each worth 1 point

For Level 1 questions, fill in the space next to the correct answer in your own Workbook.

1. What do humans depend on to survive?
   ○ a. Government
   ○ b. Environment
   ○ c. Harvesting of coal products
   ○ d. Recycling of products

Fluency Practice: Standardized Test, continued

Name _____ Date _____

2. Which of the following does the passage say plays a big role in Earth's ecosystem?
   ○ a. Forest activity   ○ c. Human activity
   ○ b. Plant activity   ○ d. Animal activity

3. Which group formed in 1971 to raise public awareness about the bad effects humans have on the ecosystem?
   ○ a. Greenpeace
   ○ b. Humans Against Pollution
   ○ c. World Assist
   ○ d. People for Pure Environments

4. Which type of ecosystem is home to more organisms than any other type of ecosystem?
   ○ a. Coral reefs   ○ c. Deserts
   ○ b. Forests   ○ d. Grasslands

5. What does Greenpeace support?
   ○ a. The destruction of forests
   ○ b. Increased paper production
   ○ c. Increased logging
   ○ d. The replanting of forests

6. Humans can reduce the bad effects they have on climate change by
   ○ a. using plastic rather than paper bags at the grocery store.
   ○ b. using coal to burn for heat and electricity.
   ○ c. drinking bottled water.
   ○ d. using less energy.

Level 2: "Understand" Question—worth 2 points (2 points for correct answer, 1 point for partially correct answer, 0 points for incorrect answer)

For the Level 2 question, write the answer in the space provided in your own Workbook.

7. Describe <u>two</u> ways human activity can change the ecosystem. What can these changes affect?

   _____

   _____

   _____

   _____

Description-or-List Chart

Name _____ Date _____

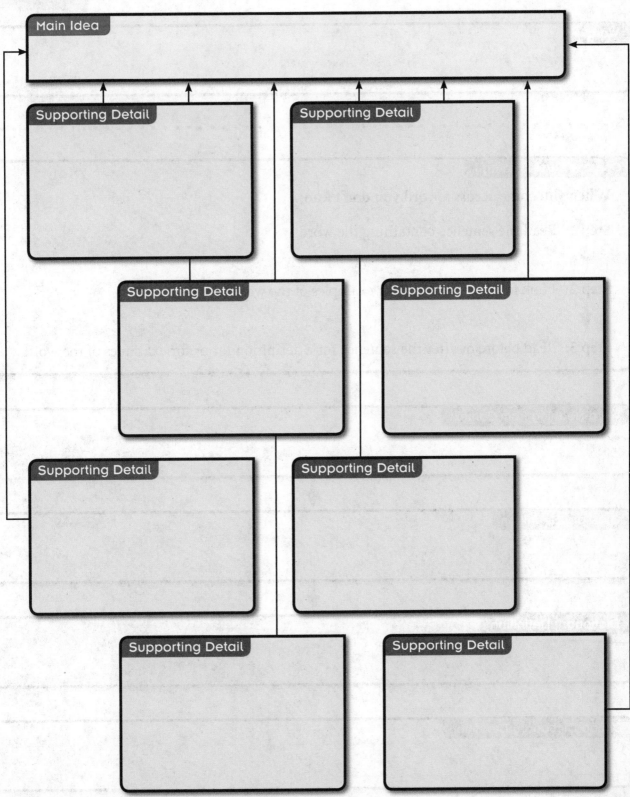

Main Idea

Supporting Detail

Supporting Detail

Supporting Detail

Supporting Detail

Supporting Detail

Supporting Detail

Supporting Detail

Supporting Detail

Lesson
4

Word-Learning Strategies

Name _____ Date _____

Word

· ·

Context-Clues Strategy

When you come across a word you don't know,

Step 1: Read the sentence containing the word.

Step 2: Look for a definition or for examples of the word in the sentence.

Step 3: Read before or after the sentence for a definition for or for examples of the word.

Word Meaning from Context

Glossary Definition

Dictionary Definition

Online-Dictionary Definition

Fluency Practice: Information Learned
Defenders of Earth's Ecosystems

Name _____ Date _____

Human Impact

Humans, like all living things, depend on the environment for survival. We need soil to grow food, water to drink, and air to breathe. We need other resources to provide shelter. We use resources for fuel to provide electricity and heat for our homes. We use resources to power cars and other vehicles.

Human activity plays a big role in Earth's ecosystems. Cutting down forests and burning fossil fuels are just two things that can change ecosystems. These changes can affect habitats, climate, and food webs in an ecosystem. Many species are unable to survive these changes.

Greenpeace Takes Action

People began to notice the bad effects humans have on ecosystems. Groups formed to raise public awareness about these problems. In 1971, Greenpeace was founded to draw attention to issues that affect Earth's ecosystems. Today, millions of people around the world assist Greenpeace.

Forests

Greenpeace supports efforts to protect forests around the world. Forests are home to more organisms than any other type of ecosystem. Forests provide oxygen and lumber. Tree roots prevent soil from washing away.

Greenpeace works to protect forests by encouraging forest-friendly practices and speaking out against activities that harm forests. Greenpeace works to stop logging practices that destroy ancient forests. It also supports the replanting of forests. Greenpeace promotes the harvesting of forest products that don't require cutting down trees. These products include fruits, nuts, rubber, and medicinal extracts.

The Future

Human activities threaten many of Earth's ecosystems, but it is possible to slow this process. Greenpeace urges people to limit their use of natural resources. Using less energy may slow climate change.

. . . .

Directions: Write three things you learned from reading the fluency passage.

1. I learned _____

_____

2. I learned _____

_____

3. I learned _____

_____

Lesson
5

Think-Pair-Share

Name _____ Date _____

Directions: Use the Think-Pair-Share Strategy to complete the question below.

Step 1: Think about the question for one minute.

Step 2: Pair and complete the question with your partner.

Step 3: Share what you wrote with the class.

Analyze

Suppose you're a sociologist who examines how groups of people interact with one another. Use your knowledge of competition and cooperation to *analyze* how people's basic needs for food, water, air, and space are affected by people's interactions.

Word-Learning Strategies

Name _____ Date _____

Word

....

Context-Clues Strategy

When you come across a word you don't know,

Step 1: Read the sentence containing the word.

Step 2: Look for a definition or for examples of the word in the sentence.

Step 3: Read before or after the sentence for a definition or for examples of the word.

Word Meaning from Context

Glossary Definition

Dictionary Definition

Online-Dictionary Definition

Lesson 2

SQ3R-Strategy Checklist

Name _____ Date _____

	Yes
Survey	
Step 1: Make text connections. **1:** What's the topic of the lesson? **2:** What's your purpose for reading? **3:** What do you know about the topic?	
Step 2: Read the beginning of the lesson.	
Step 3: Look at the main part of the lesson.	
Step 4: Read the end of the lesson.	
Question	
One section at a time, change the lesson title, subheads, or bold and highlighted words into *who, what, where, when, why,* or *how* questions.	
Read	
One section at a time, read any question, and write the answer. Reread, and adjust reading rate as needed.	
Reflect	
Step 1: Reread your notes.	
Step 2: Think about how the topic relates to you, your world, and other things you've read.	
Review	
Step 1: Read the questions. Say the answers.	
Step 2: Read the answers. Say the questions.	

Word-Learning Strategies

Name _____ Date _____

Word

- -

Context-Clues Strategy

When you come across a word you don't know,

Step 1: Read the sentence containing the word.

Step 2: Look for a definition or for examples of the word in the sentence.

Step 3: Read before or after the sentence for a definition or for examples of the word.

Word Meaning from Context

Glossary Definition

Dictionary Definition

Online-Dictionary Definition

Fluency Practice: Decoding Multipart Words

Name _____ Date _____

Nuclear Power: Outdated or the Wave of the Future?

The Origin of Nuclear Power

In 1945, the United States dropped two atomic bombs on Japan to end World War Two. After the war, the United States and other nations developed peaceful uses for nuclear energy. Nuclear power plants were built to generate electricity. Since 1950, more than a hundred nuclear power plants have operated in the United States.

The Pros and Cons of Nuclear Energy

Nuclear power generates large amounts of electricity without the use of fossil fuels. Traditional power plants burn coal or oil to make electricity. The burning of fossil fuels produces pollution. It may contribute to global warming. For this reason, many people see nuclear power as a "clean" source of energy.

However, the waste produced by nuclear energy is toxic and difficult to store safely. Nuclear waste can take hundreds of years to break down. During that time, it can contaminate soil and water supplies. Large-scale accidents have occurred at nuclear power plants. These have caused death, injury, and illness to many people who lived near these plants. Nuclear power is still used today, but many people oppose it. They feel it's unsafe for humans and the environment. A few countries plan to phase out their use of nuclear energy.

Nuclear Power Popular Again

Nuclear power has been making headlines recently. The growing concern over global warming has prompted many people to think again about this source of power. Many people worry that if nuclear power is no longer used to generate electricity, more fossil fuels will be burned to meet demand. Scientists are working to develop new and cleaner ways to make electricity. Meanwhile, many believe we should continue to use nuclear power.

Today, there are more than four hundred nuclear power plants in thirty countries. France and Finland are among the countries thinking of increasing their use of nuclear energy. In the United States, public opinion polls show people are more willing to accept nuclear power.

Strategy Steps

Step 1: Underline all the vowel sounds.

Step 2: Make a slash between the word parts so each part has one vowel sound.

Step 3: Go back to the beginning of the word, and read the parts in order.

Step 4: Read the whole word.

Word 1

Word 2

SQ3R-Strategy Checklist

Name _____ Date _____

	Yes
Survey	

Step 1: Make text connections.
    1: What's the topic of the lesson?
    2: What's your purpose for reading?
    3: What do you know about the topic?	

Step 2: Read the beginning of the lesson.	
Step 3: Look at the main part of the lesson.	
Step 4: Read the end of the lesson.	
Question	
One section at a time, change the lesson title, subheads, or bold and highlighted words into *who, what, where, when, why,* or *how* questions.	
Read	
One section at a time, read any question, and write the answer. Reread, and adjust reading rate as needed.	
Reflect	
Step 1: Reread your notes.	
Step 2: Think about how the topic relates to you, your world, and other things you've read.	
Review	
Step 1: Read the questions. Say the answers.	
Step 2: Read the answers. Say the questions.	

Lesson 3

Word-Learning Strategies

Name _____ Date _____

Word

· ·

Context-Clues Strategy

When you come across a word you don't know,

Step 1: Read the sentence containing the word.

Step 2: Look for a definition or for examples of the word in the sentence.

Step 3: Read before or after the sentence for a definition or for examples of the word.

Word Meaning from Context

Glossary Definition

Dictionary Definition

Online-Dictionary Definition

Lesson 3

Fluency Practice: Standardized Test

Name _____ Date _____

Nuclear Power: Outdated or the Wave of the Future?

The Origin of Nuclear Power

In 1945, the United States dropped two atomic bombs on Japan to end World War Two. After the war, the United States and other nations developed peaceful uses for nuclear energy. Nuclear power plants were built to generate electricity. Since 1950, more than a hundred nuclear power plants have operated in the United States.

The Pros and Cons of Nuclear Energy

Nuclear power generates large amounts of electricity without the use of fossil fuels. Traditional power plants burn coal or oil to make electricity. The burning of fossil fuels produces pollution. It may contribute to global warming. For this reason, many people see nuclear power as a "clean" source of energy.

However, the waste produced by nuclear energy is toxic and difficult to store safely. Nuclear waste can take hundreds of years to break down. During that time, it can contaminate soil and water supplies. Large-scale accidents have occurred at nuclear power plants. These have caused death, injury, and illness to many people who lived near these plants. Nuclear power is still used today, but many people oppose it. They feel it's unsafe for humans and the environment. A few countries plan to phase out their use of nuclear energy.

Nuclear Power Popular Again

Nuclear power has been making headlines recently. The growing concern over global warming has prompted many people to think again about this source of power. Many people worry that if nuclear power is no longer used to generate electricity, more fossil fuels will be burned to meet demand. Scientists are working to develop new and cleaner ways to make electricity. Meanwhile, many believe we should continue to use nuclear power.

Today, there are more than four hundred nuclear power plants in thirty countries. France and Finland are among the countries thinking of increasing their use of nuclear energy. In the United States, public opinion polls show people are more willing to accept nuclear power.

Score _____ /8 = _____ %

Directions: Take turns reading the questions. Answer the questions together.

Level 1: "Remember" Questions—each worth 1 point

For Level 1 questions, fill in the space next to the correct answer in your own Workbook.

1. After World War II, the United States built nuclear power plants to
   - ○ a. create new jobs for people.
   - ○ c. generate electricity.
   - ○ b. make atomic bombs.
   - ○ d. discover fossil fuels.

Lesson 3

Fluency Practice: Standardized Test, continued

Name _____ Date _____

2. According to the passage, traditional power plants
  ○ a. use wind power.
  ○ b. do not use fossil fuels.
  ○ c. do not produce pollution.
  ○ d. may contribute to global warming.

3. How long can it take to break down nuclear waste?
  ○ a. Thousands of years
  ○ b. Hundreds of years
  ○ c. A few dozen years
  ○ d. Only ten years

4. Nuclear waste
  ○ a. is toxic.
  ○ b. is safe.
  ○ c. is beneficial.
  ○ d. never breaks down.

5. The passage suggests that nuclear power plants are
  ○ a. a safe source of energy.
  ○ b. a source of air pollution.
  ○ c. a clean source of energy.
  ○ d. an outdated fuel source.

6. In the United States, public opinion polls show that
  ○ a. people are unsure if they're willing to accept nuclear power.
  ○ b. people are more willing to accept nuclear power.
  ○ c. people prefer to use coal to make electricity.
  ○ d. people are less willing to accept nuclear power.

Level 2: "Understand" Question—worth 2 points (2 points for correct answer, 1 point for partially correct answer, 0 points for incorrect answer)

For the Level 2 question, write the answer in the space provided in your own Workbook.

7. Explain why many people consider nuclear power a "clean" source of energy.

_____

_____

_____

Lesson 4

SQ3R-Strategy Checklist

Name _____ Date _____

	Yes
Survey	
Step 1: Make text connections. **1:** What's the topic of the lesson? **2:** What's your purpose for reading? **3:** What do you know about the topic?	
Step 2: Read the beginning of the lesson.	
Step 3: Look at the main part of the lesson.	
Step 4: Read the end of the lesson.	
Question	
One section at a time, change the lesson title, subheads, or bold and highlighted words into *who, what, where, when, why,* or *how* questions.	
Read	
One section at a time, read any question, and write the answer. Reread, and adjust reading rate as needed.	
Reflect	
Step 1: Reread your notes.	
Step 2: Think about how the topic relates to you, your world, and other things you've read.	
Review	
Step 1: Read the questions. Say the answers.	
Step 2: Read the answers. Say the questions.	

Cause-and-Effect Chart

Name _____ Date _____

Cause		Effect

Cause		Effect

Cause		Effect

Lesson 4

Word-Learning Strategies

Name _____ Date _____

Word

Context-Clues Strategy

When you come across a word you don't know,

Step 1: Read the sentence containing the word.

Step 2: Look for a definition or for examples of the word in the sentence.

Step 3: Read before or after the sentence for a definition or for examples of the word.

Word Meaning from Context

Glossary Definition

Dictionary Definition

Online-Dictionary Definition

Fluency Practice: Information Learned

Name _____ Date _____

Nuclear Power: Outdated or the Wave of the Future?

The Origin of Nuclear Power

In 1945, the United States dropped two atomic bombs on Japan to end World War Two. After the war, the United States and other nations developed peaceful uses for nuclear energy. Nuclear power plants were built to generate electricity. Since 1950, more than a hundred nuclear power plants have operated in the United States.

The Pros and Cons of Nuclear Energy

Nuclear power generates large amounts of electricity without the use of fossil fuels. Traditional power plants burn coal or oil to make electricity. The burning of fossil fuels produces pollution. It may contribute to global warming. For this reason, many people see nuclear power as a "clean" source of energy.

However, the waste produced by nuclear energy is toxic and difficult to store safely. Nuclear waste can take hundreds of years to break down. During that time, it can contaminate soil and water supplies. Large-scale accidents have occurred at nuclear power plants. These have caused death, injury, and illness to many people who lived near these plants. Nuclear power is still used today, but many people oppose it. They feel it's unsafe for humans and the environment. A few countries plan to phase out their use of nuclear energy.

Nuclear Power Popular Again

Nuclear power has been making headlines recently. The growing concern over global warming has prompted many people to think again about this source of power. Many people worry that if nuclear power is no longer used to generate electricity, more fossil fuels will be burned to meet demand. Scientists are working to develop new and cleaner ways to make electricity. Meanwhile, many believe we should continue to use nuclear power.

Today, there are more than four hundred nuclear power plants in thirty countries. France and Finland are among the countries thinking of increasing their use of nuclear energy. In the United States, public opinion polls show people are more willing to accept nuclear power.

Directions: Write three things you learned from reading the fluency passage.

1. I learned _____

_____

2. I learned _____

_____

3. I learned _____

_____

Lesson

5

Think-Pair-Share

Name _____ Date _____

Directions: Use the Think-Pair-Share Strategy to complete the question below.

Step 1: **Think** about the question for one minute.

Step 2: **Pair** and complete the question with your partner.

Step 3: **Share** what you wrote with the class.

Analyze

Suppose you're a chef cooking soup in a large, covered pot. You've noticed that water drips off the inside of the lid when you lift the lid to check the soup. Use your knowledge of changes in states of matter to *analyze* why this happens.

SQ3R-Strategy Checklist

Name _____ Date _____

	Yes
Survey	
Step 1: Make text connections. 1: What's the topic of the lesson? 2: What's your purpose for reading? 3: What do you know about the topic?	
Step 2: Read the beginning of the lesson.	
Step 3: Look at the main part of the lesson.	
Step 4: Read the end of the lesson.	
Question	
One section at a time, change the lesson title, subheads, or bold and highlighted words into *who, what, where, when, why,* or *how* questions.	
Read	
One section at a time, read any question, and write the answer. Reread, and adjust reading rate as needed.	
Reflect	
Step 1: Reread your notes.	
Step 2: Think about how the topic relates to you, your world, and other things you've read.	
Review	
Step 1: Read the questions. Say the answers.	
Step 2: Read the answers. Say the questions.	

Lesson 1

Word-Learning Strategies

Name _____ Date _____

Word

. . . .

Context-Clues Strategy

When you come across a word you don't know,

Step 1: Read the sentence containing the word.

Step 2: Look for a definition or for examples of the word in the sentence.

Step 3: Read before or after the sentence for a definition or for examples of the word.

Word Meaning from Context

Glossary Definition

Dictionary Definition

Online-Dictionary Definition

Lesson 2

Activity 1

SQ3R-Strategy Checklist

Name _____ Date _____

	Yes
Survey	
Step 1: Make text connections. 1: What's the topic of the lesson? 2: What's your purpose for reading? 3: What do you know about the topic?	
Step 2: Read the beginning of the lesson.	
Step 3: Look at the main part of the lesson.	
Step 4: Read the end of the lesson.	
Question	
One section at a time, change the lesson title, subheads, or bold and highlighted words into *who, what, where, when, why,* or *how* questions.	
Read	
One section at a time, read any question, and write the answer. Reread, and adjust reading rate as needed.	
Reflect	
Step 1: Reread your notes.	
Step 2: Think about how the topic relates to you, your world, and other things you've read.	
Review	
Step 1: Read the questions. Say the answers.	
Step 2: Read the answers. Say the questions.	

Note-Taking Form

Name _____ Date _____

Question (Page Number)	**Answer**

Lesson
2

Word-Learning Strategies

Name _____ Date _____

Word

- -

Context-Clues Strategy

When you come across a word you don't know,

Step 1: Read the sentence containing the word.

Step 2: Look for a definition or for examples of the word in the sentence.

Step 3: Read before or after the sentence for a definition or for examples of the word.

Word Meaning from Context

Glossary Definition

Dictionary Definition

Online-Dictionary Definition

Lesson 2

Fluency Practice: Decoding Multipart Words

Name _____ Date _____

The Fall of the Berlin Wall

In May 1945, the Allied side is winning World War II. Soviet troops capture Berlin, the German capital, and soon after, the city is divided. The French, the British, and the Americans occupy the west side. The Soviets occupy the east.

Eight years later, the former allies are enemies. The Soviet Union controls Eastern Europe, including East Germany, and the puppet governments in these countries forbid their people to visit the West. The one exception is Berlin. East Berliners can still cross into West Berlin. West Berlin is an island of opportunity outside the German-run government in Communist-controlled East Germany. In contrast, East Berliners receive low wages and are subject to harsh laws passed in the Soviet Union. In June 1953, thousands of East Berliners protest in the streets. Soviet tanks push back the crowds, and forty people die.

Another eight years pass. East Berlin's Communist leaders erect a wall between East and West Berlin. Armed guards with dogs patrol the entire length, and East Berliners who try to go over or under the Berlin wall are shot.

Fast-forward to 1989. Hungary is breaking away from the Soviets. In September, the Hungarian government stops restricting East German travel. Thousands of East Germans go through Hungary to West Germany.

The Germans who stay behind hold weekly protests. On November 4, a million protesters turn out in East Berlin. In response, the hard-line Communists in the East German government step down.

The government announces that people are free to go in and out of East Berlin. At midnight on November 9, the first crowds of East Berliners pass through the wall's gates. West Berliners greet them with cheers and whistles and hand out German money. (East German marks are worthless outside East Germany.)

For weeks afterward, people arrive at the wall to pound it with hammers and picks. Whole chunks disappear, and later, some bricks turn up in sculptures in faraway cities such as Paris and New York. Today, all that remains are two rows of paving bricks that mark the location of the Berlin wall.

Strategy Steps

Step 1: Underline all the vowel sounds.

Step 2: Make a slash between the word parts so each part has one vowel sound.

Step 3: Go back to the beginning of the word, and read the parts in order.

Step 4: Read the whole word.

Word 1

Word 2

SQ3R-Strategy Checklist

Name _____ Date _____

	Yes
Survey	
Step 1: Make text connections. 1: What's the topic of the lesson? 2: What's your purpose for reading? 3: What do you know about the topic?	
Step 2: Read the beginning of the lesson.	
Step 3: Look at the main part of the lesson.	
Step 4: Read the end of the lesson.	
Question	
One section at a time, change the lesson title, subheads, or bold and highlighted words into *who, what, where, when, why,* or *how* questions.	
Read	
One section at a time, read any question, and write the answer. Reread, and adjust reading rate as needed.	
Reflect	
Step 1: Reread your notes.	
Step 2: Think about how the topic relates to you, your world, and other things you've read.	
Review	
Step 1: Read the questions. Say the answers.	
Step 2: Read the answers. Say the questions.	

Note-Taking Form

Name _____ Date _____

Question (Page Number)	Answer

Lesson
3

Word-Learning Strategies

Name _____ Date _____

Word

. . . .

Context-Clues Strategy

When you come across a word you don't know,

Step 1: Read the sentence containing the word.

Step 2: Look for a definition or for examples of the word in the sentence.

Step 3: Read before or after the sentence for a definition or for examples of the word.

Word Meaning from Context

Glossary Definition

Dictionary Definition

Online-Dictionary Definition

Lesson 3

Fluency Practice: Standardized Test

Name _____ Date _____

The Fall of the Berlin Wall

In May 1945, the Allied side is winning World War II. Soviet troops capture Berlin, the German capital, and soon after, the city is divided. The French, the British, and the Americans occupy the west side. The Soviets occupy the east.

Eight years later, the former allies are enemies. The Soviet Union controls Eastern Europe, including East Germany, and the puppet governments in these countries forbid their people to visit the West. The one exception is Berlin. East Berliners can still cross into West Berlin. West Berlin is an island of opportunity outside the German-run government in Communist-controlled East Germany. In contrast, East Berliners receive low wages and are subject to harsh laws passed in the Soviet Union. In June 1953, thousands of East Berliners protest in the streets. Soviet tanks push back the crowds, and forty people die.

Another eight years pass. East Berlin's Communist leaders erect a wall between East and West Berlin. Armed guards with dogs patrol the entire length, and East Berliners who try to go over or under the Berlin wall are shot.

Fast-forward to 1989. Hungary is breaking away from the Soviets. In September, the Hungarian government stops restricting East German travel. Thousands of East Germans go through Hungary to West Germany.

The Germans who stay behind hold weekly protests. On November 4, a million protesters turn out in East Berlin. In response, the hard-line Communists in the East German government step down.

The government announces that people are free to go in and out of East Berlin. At midnight on November 9, the first crowds of East Berliners pass through the wall's gates. West Berliners greet them with cheers and whistles and hand out German money. (East German marks are worthless outside East Germany.)

For weeks afterward, people arrive at the wall to pound it with hammers and picks. Whole chunks disappear, and later, some bricks turn up in sculptures in faraway cities such as Paris and New York. Today, all that remains are two rows of paving bricks that mark the location of the Berlin wall.

Score _____ /8 = _____ %

Directions: Take turns reading the questions. Answer the questions together.

Level 1: "Remember" Questions—each worth 1 point

For Level 1 questions, fill in the space next to the correct answer in your own Workbook.

1. After Berlin was captured and divided, which side did the Soviets occupy?
   - ○ a. East
   - ○ b. North
   - ○ c. South
   - ○ d. Central

Lesson 3

Fluency Practice: Standardized Test, continued

Name _____ Date _____

2. Which of these is true about Berlin before 1953?
   ○ a. Neither East nor West Berliners could cross into each other's countries.
   ○ b. East and West Berliners could still cross into each other's countries.
   ○ c. East Berliners could still cross into West Berlin.
   ○ d. Only government officials could visit West Berlin.

3. Why did thousands of East Berliners protest in the streets in 1953?
   ○ a. They wanted more cars.
   ○ b. They received low wages and were subject to harsh laws.
   ○ c. There was a shortage of food.
   ○ d. People were being unlawfully imprisoned for visiting West Berlin.

4. East Berlin's Communist leaders
   ○ a. declared war on West Berlin.
   ○ b. made allies with West Berlin.
   ○ c. built a wall between East and West Berlin.
   ○ d. built a chain-link fence between East and West Berlin.

5. Which country did East Germans travel through to get to West Germany in 1989?
   ○ a. Turkey   ○ c. Poland
   ○ b. Hungary   ○ d. Paris

6. What happened at midnight on November 9, 1989?
   ○ a. The first crowds of East Berliners passed through the gates into West Berlin.
   ○ b. East Berlin's government ordered that an even higher wall be built between East and West Berlin.
   ○ c. West Berlin became a Communist government like East Berlin.
   ○ d. Soviet tanks prevented people from crossing back to West Berlin.

Level 2: "Understand" Question—worth 2 points (2 points for correct answer, 1 point for partially correct answer, 0 points for incorrect answer)

For the Level 2 question, write the answer in the space provided in your own Workbook.

7. Explain why East Berlin's Communist leaders built the Berlin wall.

_____

_____

_____

_____

_____

Lesson 4

SQ3R-Strategy Checklist

Name _____ Date _____

	Yes
Survey	
Step 1: Make text connections. **1:** What's the topic of the lesson? **2:** What's your purpose for reading? **3:** What do you know about the topic?	
Step 2: Read the beginning of the lesson.	
Step 3: Look at the main part of the lesson.	
Step 4: Read the end of the lesson.	
Question	
One section at a time, change the lesson title, subheads, or bold and highlighted words into *who, what, where, when, why,* or *how* questions.	
Read	
One section at a time, read any question, and write the answer. Reread, and adjust reading rate as needed.	
Reflect	
Step 1: Reread your notes.	
Step 2: Think about how the topic relates to you, your world, and other things you've read.	
Review	
Step 1: Read the questions. Say the answers.	
Step 2: Read the answers. Say the questions.	

Note-Taking Form

Name _____ Date _____

Question (Page Number)	**Answer**

Lesson 4

Compare-and-Contrast Chart

Name _____ Date _____

Different	Same	Different

Lesson
4

Word-Learning Strategies

Name _____ Date _____

Word

· ·

Context-Clues Strategy

When you come across a word you don't know,

Step 1: Read the sentence containing the word.

Step 2: Look for a definition or for examples of the word in the sentence.

Step 3: Read before or after the sentence for a definition or for examples of the word.

Word Meaning from Context

Glossary Definition

Dictionary Definition

Online-Dictionary Definition

Lesson 4

Fluency Practice: Information Learned

Name _____ Date _____

The Fall of the Berlin Wall

In May 1945, the Allied side is winning World War II. Soviet troops capture Berlin, the German capital, and soon after, the city is divided. The French, the British, and the Americans occupy the west side. The Soviets occupy the east.

Eight years later, the former allies are enemies. The Soviet Union controls Eastern Europe, including East Germany, and the puppet governments in these countries forbid their people to visit the West. The one exception is Berlin. East Berliners can still cross into West Berlin. West Berlin is an island of opportunity outside the German-run government in Communist-controlled East Germany. In contrast, East Berliners receive low wages and are subject to harsh laws passed in the Soviet Union. In June 1953, thousands of East Berliners protest in the streets. Soviet tanks push back the crowds, and forty people die.

Another eight years pass. East Berlin's Communist leaders erect a wall between East and West Berlin. Armed guards with dogs patrol the entire length, and East Berliners who try to go over or under the Berlin wall are shot.

Fast-forward to 1989. Hungary is breaking away from the Soviets. In September, the Hungarian government stops restricting East German travel. Thousands of East Germans go through Hungary to West Germany.

The Germans who stay behind hold weekly protests. On November 4, a million protesters turn out in East Berlin. In response, the hard-line Communists in the East German government step down.

The government announces that people are free to go in and out of East Berlin. At midnight on November 9, the first crowds of East Berliners pass through the wall's gates. West Berliners greet them with cheers and whistles and hand out German money. (East German marks are worthless outside East Germany.)

For weeks afterward, people arrive at the wall to pound it with hammers and picks. Whole chunks disappear, and later, some bricks turn up in sculptures in faraway cities such as Paris and New York. Today, all that remains are two rows of paving bricks that mark the location of the Berlin wall.

Directions: Write three things you learned from reading the fluency passage.

1. I learned _____

_____

2. I learned _____

_____

3. I learned _____

_____

Lesson 5

Think-Pair-Share

Name _____ Date _____

Directions

Directions: Use the Think-Pair-Share Strategy to complete the question below.

Step 1: **Think** about the question for one minute.

Step 2: **Pair** and complete the question with your partner.

Step 3: **Share** what you wrote with the class.

Analyze

Suppose you're a volunteer working with Brazilian farmers to improve current agricultural methods. Use your knowledge of the effects of slash-and-burn methods to *analyze* alternatives that will lessen the negative impact of slash-and-burn methods on both the environment and the lives of farmers.

SQ3R-Strategy Checklist

Name _____ Date _____

	Yes
Survey	
Step 1: Make text connections. **1:** What's the topic of the lesson? **2:** What's your purpose for reading? **3:** What do you know about the topic?	
Step 2: Read the beginning of the lesson.	
Step 3: Look at the main part of the lesson.	
Step 4: Read the end of the lesson.	
Question	
One section at a time, change the lesson title, subheads, or bold and highlighted words into *who, what, where, when, why,* or *how* questions.	
Read	
One section at a time, read any question, and write the answer. Reread, and adjust reading rate as needed.	
Reflect	
Step 1: Reread your notes.	
Step 2: Think about how the topic relates to you, your world, and other things you've read.	
Review	
Step 1: Read the questions. Say the answers.	
Step 2: Read the answers. Say the questions.	

Lesson
1

Note-Taking Form

Name _____ Date _____

Question (Page Number)	Answer

Lesson 1

Word-Learning Strategies

Name _____ Date _____

Word

· ·

Context-Clues Strategy

When you come across a word you don't know,

Step 1: Read the sentence containing the word.

Step 2: Look for a definition or for examples of the word in the sentence.

Step 3: Read before or after the sentence for a definition or for examples of the word.

Word Meaning from Context

Glossary Definition

Dictionary Definition

Online-Dictionary Definition

Lesson
2

SQ3R-Strategy Checklist

Name _____ Date _____

	Yes
Survey	

Step 1: Make text connections.
    1: What's the topic of the lesson?
    2: What's your purpose for reading?
    3: What do you know about the topic?	

Step 2: Read the beginning of the lesson.	
Step 3: Look at the main part of the lesson.	
Step 4: Read the end of the lesson.	
Question	
One section at a time, change the lesson title, subheads, or bold and highlighted words into *who, what, where, when, why,* or *how* questions.	
Read	
One section at a time, read any question, and write the answer. Reread, and adjust reading rate as needed.	
Reflect	
Step 1: Reread your notes.	
Step 2: Think about how the topic relates to you, your world, and other things you've read.	
Review	
Step 1: Read the questions. Say the answers.	
Step 2: Read the answers. Say the questions.	

Lesson 2

Note-Taking Form

Name _____ Date _____

Question (Page Number)	Answer

Lesson 2

Word-Learning Strategies

Name _____ Date _____

Word

- -

Context-Clues Strategy

When you come across a word you don't know,

Step 1: Read the sentence containing the word.

Step 2: Look for a definition or for examples of the word in the sentence.

Step 3: Read before or after the sentence for a definition or for examples of the word.

Word Meaning from Context

Glossary Definition

Dictionary Definition

Online-Dictionary Definition

Lesson 2

Fluency Practice: Decoding Multipart Words

Name _____ Date _____

The Fire Knife Dance

Welcome to the Samoa Festival. Each year, high school students from all over Polynesia show off their skill in traditional arts. Some make speeches. Others compete in basket weaving, coconut husking, fire making, and more. Hear those drums. Follow the beat to the fire knife dancers.

Fire knife dances are based on ancient victory celebrations of Samoan warriors. After a battle, the warriors would wave a wooden weapon known as the *nifo oti,* or "deadly tooth." Long after Samoans left war behind, villagers would twirl *nifo oti* in welcome ceremonies for special guests. Samoans still use a hooked version of the knife to celebrate important occasions.

Over time, young Samoans rehearsed *nifo oti* movements and developed complex routines, often with two or three knives. The most exciting innovation came in 1946. A performer named Uluao Letuli added flames to both ends of his *nifo oti.* Today, Letuli is known as the father of Samoan fire knife dancing.

Successful fire knife dancers need the combined skills of a Samoan warrior, a Hindu fire-eater, and an American baton twirler. They practice constantly with fire and sharp blades. Still, they're often burned and cut. The potential danger adds to the drama of the dance.

Music also adds to the drama. Fire knife dancers move to drum beats. A favorite accompaniment is the traditional slit-log drum. This is a hollowed-out section of a tree. It ranges in size from one foot in length to a complete tree trunk. Other fire knife drummers bang on small metal tins and large oil drums. Fire knife dancers favor rapid rhythms that underscore their speed and daring.

The dancers' costumes are part of the spectacle. Most dancers wear a *lavalava*—a cloth wrapped around the waist and tucked between the legs. Anything more flowing might snag on the knives or catch fire. Some dancers wear bands of leaves on their wrists and ankles to draw attention to the movements of their arms and legs. Most people in the audience, however, cannot take their eyes off the flames.

Strategy Steps

Step 1: Underline all the vowel sounds.

Step 2: Make a slash between the word parts so each part has one vowel sound.

Step 3: Go back to the beginning of the word, and read the parts in order.

Step 4: Read the whole word.

Word 1

Word 2

SQ3R-Strategy Checklist

Name _____ Date _____

	Yes
Survey	
Step 1: Make text connections. 1: What's the topic of the lesson? 2: What's your purpose for reading? 3: What do you know about the topic?	
Step 2: Read the beginning of the lesson.	
Step 3: Look at the main part of the lesson.	
Step 4: Read the end of the lesson.	
Question	
One section at a time, change the lesson title, subheads, or bold and highlighted words into *who, what, where, when, why,* or *how* questions.	
Read	
One section at a time, read any question, and write the answer. Reread, and adjust reading rate as needed.	
Reflect	
Step 1: Reread your notes.	
Step 2: Think about how the topic relates to you, your world, and other things you've read.	
Review	
Step 1: Read the questions. Say the answers.	
Step 2: Read the answers. Say the questions.	

Lesson
3

Note-Taking Form

Name _____ Date _____

Question (Page Number)	Answer

Word-Learning Strategies

Name _____ Date _____

Word

· ·

Context-Clues Strategy

When you come across a word you don't know,

Step 1: Read the sentence containing the word.

Step 2: Look for a definition or for examples of the word in the sentence.

Step 3: Read before or after the sentence for a definition or for examples of the word.

Word Meaning from Context

Glossary Definition

Dictionary Definition

Online-Dictionary Definition

Lesson 3

Fluency Practice: Standardized Test

Name _____ Date _____

The Fire Knife Dance

Welcome to the Samoa Festival. Each year, high school students from all over Polynesia show off their skill in traditional arts. Some make speeches. Others compete in basket weaving, coconut husking, fire making, and more. Hear those drums. Follow the beat to the fire knife dancers.

Fire knife dances are based on ancient victory celebrations of Samoan warriors. After a battle, the warriors would wave a wooden weapon known as the *nifo oti,* or "deadly tooth." Long after Samoans left war behind, villagers would twirl *nifo oti* in welcome ceremonies for special guests. Samoans still use a hooked version of the knife to celebrate important occasions.

Over time, young Samoans rehearsed *nifo oti* movements and developed complex routines, often with two or three knives. The most exciting innovation came in 1946. A performer named Uluao Letuli added flames to both ends of his *nifo oti.* Today, Letuli is known as the father of Samoan fire knife dancing.

Successful fire knife dancers need the combined skills of a Samoan warrior, a Hindu fire-eater, and an American baton twirler. They practice constantly with fire and sharp blades. Still, they're often burned and cut. The potential danger adds to the drama of the dance.

Music also adds to the drama. Fire knife dancers move to drum beats. A favorite accompaniment is the traditional slit-log drum. This is a hollowed-out section of a tree. It ranges in size from one foot in length to a complete tree trunk. Other fire knife drummers bang on small metal tins and large oil drums. Fire knife dancers favor rapid rhythms that underscore their speed and daring.

The dancers' costumes are part of the spectacle. Most dancers wear a *lavalava*—a cloth wrapped around the waist and tucked between the legs. Anything more flowing might snag on the knives or catch fire. Some dancers wear bands of leaves on their wrists and ankles to draw attention to the movements of their arms and legs. Most people in the audience, however, cannot take their eyes off the flames.

Score _____ /8 = _____ %

Directions: Take turns reading the questions. Answer the questions together.

Level 1: "Remember" Questions—each worth 1 point

For Level 1 questions, fill in the space next to the correct answer in your own Workbook.

1. What are some events you would find at the Samoa Festival?
   - ○ a. Cooking and archery
   - ○ b. Basket weaving and fire making
   - ○ c. Swimming and running contests
   - ○ d. Fishing and hunting

Lesson 3

Fluency Practice: Standardized Test, continued

Name _____ Date _____

2. What are fire knife dances based on?
- ○ a. Ancient victory celebrations of warriors
- ○ b. Ancient ceremonies to celebrate births
- ○ c. Ancient celebrations to mark the changing seasons
- ○ d. Ancient meetings to discuss marriages and anniversaries

3. What does *nifo oti* mean?
- ○ a. "Hunting dance"
- ○ b. "Battle cry"
- ○ c. "Warrior costume"
- ○ d. "Deadly tooth"

4. What exciting innovation happened in 1946?
- ○ a. Larger knives were invented and were easier to throw.
- ○ b. Women were allowed to perform fire knife dances.
- ○ c. A performer added flames to his fire knife.
- ○ d. Warriors used guns rather than knives to hunt prey.

5. What is a slit-log drum made of?
- ○ a. A hollowed-out section of tree
- ○ b. A tight piece of cloth
- ○ c. A solid tree trunk
- ○ d. A cracked tree trunk

6. Most fire knife dancers wear a costume known as a
- ○ a. mumu.
- ○ b. lavalava.
- ○ c. tiki.
- ○ d. bandanna.

Level 2: "Understand" Question—worth 2 points (2 points for correct answer, 1 point for partially correct answer, 0 points for incorrect answer)

For the Level 2 question, write the answer in the space provided in your own Workbook.

7. Explain how fire knife dances started. _____

_____

_____

_____

_____

_____

Lesson 4

SQ3R-Strategy Checklist

Name _____ Date _____

	Yes
Survey	
Step 1: Make text connections. 　　　　**1:** What's the topic of the lesson? 　　　　**2:** What's your purpose for reading? 　　　　**3:** What do you know about the topic?	
Step 2: Read the beginning of the lesson.	
Step 3: Look at the main part of the lesson.	
Step 4: Read the end of the lesson.	
Question	
One section at a time, change the lesson title, subheads, or bold and highlighted words into *who, what, where, when, why,* or *how* questions.	
Read	
One section at a time, read any question, and write the answer. Reread, and adjust reading rate as needed.	
Reflect	
Step 1: Reread your notes.	
Step 2: Think about how the topic relates to you, your world, and other things you've read.	
Review	
Step 1: Read the questions. Say the answers.	
Step 2: Read the answers. Say the questions.	

Note-Taking Form

Name _____ Date _____

Question (Page Number)	Answer

Description-or-List Chart

Name _____ Date _____

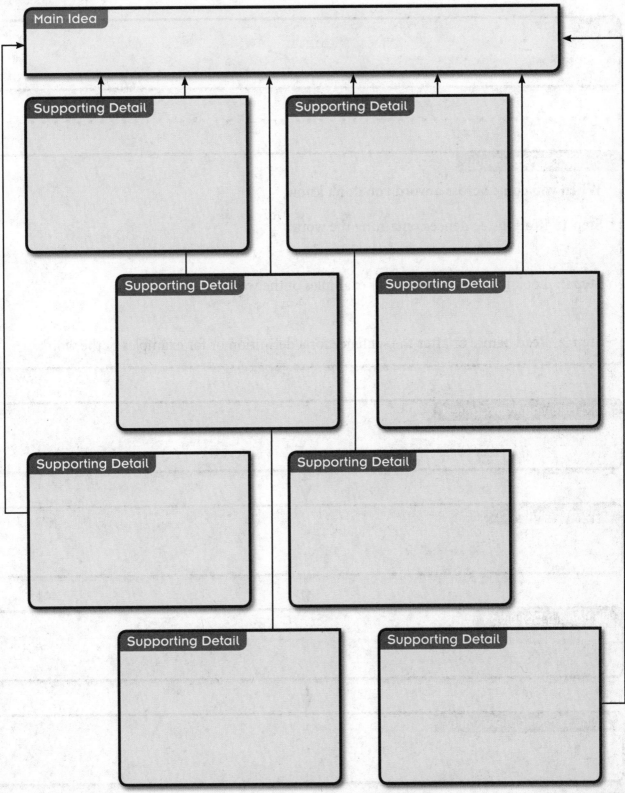

Main Idea

Supporting Detail

Supporting Detail

Supporting Detail

Supporting Detail

Supporting Detail

Supporting Detail

Supporting Detail

Supporting Detail

Word-Learning Strategies

Name _____ Date _____

Word

. . . .

Context-Clues Strategy

When you come across a word you don't know,

Step 1: Read the sentence containing the word.

Step 2: Look for a definition or for examples of the word in the sentence.

Step 3: Read before or after the sentence for a definition or for examples of the word.

Word Meaning from Context

Glossary Definition

Dictionary Definition

Online-Dictionary Definition

Lesson 4

Fluency Practice: Information Learned

Name _____ Date _____

The Fire Knife Dance

Welcome to the Samoa Festival. Each year, high school students from all over Polynesia show off their skill in traditional arts. Some make speeches. Others compete in basket weaving, coconut husking, fire making, and more. Hear those drums. Follow the beat to the fire knife dancers.

Fire knife dances are based on ancient victory celebrations of Samoan warriors. After a battle, the warriors would wave a wooden weapon known as the *nifo oti,* or "deadly tooth." Long after Samoans left war behind, villagers would twirl *nifo oti* in welcome ceremonies for special guests. Samoans still use a hooked version of the knife to celebrate important occasions.

Over time, young Samoans rehearsed *nifo oti* movements and developed complex routines, often with two or three knives. The most exciting innovation came in 1946. A performer named Uluao Letuli added flames to both ends of his *nifo oti*. Today, Letuli is known as the father of Samoan fire knife dancing.

Successful fire knife dancers need the combined skills of a Samoan warrior, a Hindu fire-eater, and an American baton twirler. They practice constantly with fire and sharp blades. Still, they're often burned and cut. The potential danger adds to the drama of the dance.

Music also adds to the drama. Fire knife dancers move to drum beats. A favorite accompaniment is the traditional slit-log drum. This is a hollowed-out section of a tree. It ranges in size from one foot in length to a complete tree trunk. Other fire knife drummers bang on small metal tins and large oil drums. Fire knife dancers favor rapid rhythms that underscore their speed and daring.

The dancers' costumes are part of the spectacle. Most dancers wear a *lavalava*—a cloth wrapped around the waist and tucked between the legs. Anything more flowing might snag on the knives or catch fire. Some dancers wear bands of leaves on their wrists and ankles to draw attention to the movements of their arms and legs. Most people in the audience, however, cannot take their eyes off the flames.

Directions: Write three things you learned from reading the fluency passage.

1. I learned _____

_____

2. I learned _____

_____

3. I learned _____

_____

Lesson
5

Think-Pair-Share

Name _____ Date _____

Directions

Directions: Use the Think-Pair-Share Strategy to complete the question below.

Step 1: **Think** about the question for one minute.

Step 2: **Pair** and complete the question with your partner.

Step 3: **Share** what you wrote with the class.

Analyze

Suppose you're a sociologist studying changes in India's caste system. *Analyze* what you know about the treatment of dalits before and after Mohandas Gandhi's leadership by comparing past treatment of dalits with current treatment of dalits.

Lesson
1

SQ3R-Strategy Checklist

Name _____ Date _____

	Yes
Survey	

Step 1: Make text connections.
     1: What's the topic of the lesson?
     2: What's your purpose for reading?
     3: What do you know about the topic?	

Step 2: Read the beginning of the lesson.	
Step 3: Look at the main part of the lesson.	
Step 4: Read the end of the lesson.	
Question	
One section at a time, change the lesson title, subheads, or bold and highlighted words into *who, what, where, when, why,* or *how* questions.	
Read	
One section at a time, read any question, and write the answer. Reread, and adjust reading rate as needed.	
Reflect	
Step 1: Reread your notes.	
Step 2: Think about how the topic relates to you, your world, and other things you've read.	
Review	
Step 1: Read the questions. Say the answers.	
Step 2: Read the answers. Say the questions.	

Note-Taking Form

Name _____ Date _____

Question (Page Number)	**Answer**

Lesson 1

Word-Learning Strategies

Name _____ Date _____

Word

....

Context-Clues Strategy

When you come across a word you don't know,

Step 1: Read the sentence containing the word.

Step 2: Look for a definition or for examples of the word in the sentence.

Step 3: Read before or after the sentence for a definition or for examples of the word.

Word Meaning from Context

Glossary Definition

Dictionary Definition

Online-Dictionary Definition

SQ3R-Strategy Checklist

Name _____ Date _____

	Yes
Survey	
Step 1: Make text connections. 　　　1: What's the topic of the lesson? 　　　2: What's your purpose for reading? 　　　3: What do you know about the topic?	
Step 2: Read the beginning of the lesson.	
Step 3: Look at the main part of the lesson.	
Step 4: Read the end of the lesson.	
Question	
One section at a time, change the lesson title, subheads, or bold and highlighted words into *who, what, where, when, why,* or *how* questions.	
Read	
One section at a time, read any question, and write the answer. Reread, and adjust reading rate as needed.	
Reflect	
Step 1: Reread your notes.	
Step 2: Think about how the topic relates to you, your world, and other things you've read.	
Review	
Step 1: Read the questions. Say the answers.	
Step 2: Read the answers. Say the questions.	

Lesson 2

Note-Taking Form

Name _____ Date _____

Question (Page Number)	**Answer**

Word-Learning Strategies

Name _____ Date _____

Word

··

Context-Clues Strategy

When you come across a word you don't know,

Step 1: Read the sentence containing the word.

Step 2: Look for a definition or for examples of the word in the sentence.

Step 3: Read before or after the sentence for a definition or for examples of the word.

Word Meaning from Context

Glossary Definition

Dictionary Definition

Online-Dictionary Definition

Fluency Practice: Decoding Multipart Words

Name _____ Date _____

Isaac Newton, Father of Physical Science

Isaac Newton was one of the most influential figures in the history of science. He invented new mathematical methods. He developed theories about light and color. He wrote laws about mechanics—the study of forces and motion. Much of his work has withstood the test of time. His laws, his theories, and his calculations still hold true.

Early Life and School Days

Newton had a difficult childhood. His father, a farmer, died before Newton was born, and Newton was sent to live with his grandmother when he was three. When he was eleven, he and his mother were reunited, and he left school to work on the farm. From all accounts, he wasn't cut out for farming, so he returned to school.

Newton was an unremarkable student. He didn't begin to realize his full potential until he entered college. At Cambridge University, he studied the teachings of ancient Greek philosophers and mathematicians. On his own, he studied the works of the greatest scientists of his time.

Contributions to Science and Mathematics

After graduation, Newton developed new methods in calculus, a branch of mathematics that plays an important role in physical science. Legend says that during this time Newton observed a falling apple while sitting in an orchard. According to the story, this observation began Newton's study of gravity.

Newton conducted many experiments with light and color. He used prisms to separate white light into the colors of the spectrum. Newton theorized that light travels in straight lines instead of waves. Newton detailed his work in a three-volume work called *Opticks*.

Twenty years of study and experimentation resulted in *Principia*, one of the most important scientific works ever published. Book I details his theories about motion and force, including his three laws of motion. Book II is about the motion of fluids. Book III explains the motion of planets and their moons by the force of gravity. Newton united objects on Earth and in space under one set of laws.

Strategy Steps

Step 1: Underline all the vowel sounds.

Step 2: Make a slash between the word parts so each part has one vowel sound.

Step 3: Go back to the beginning of the word, and read the parts in order.

Step 4: Read the whole word.

Word 1

Word 2

SQ3R-Strategy Checklist

Name _____ Date _____

	Yes
Survey	
Step 1: Make text connections. 1: What's the topic of the lesson? 2: What's your purpose for reading? 3: What do you know about the topic?	
Step 2: Read the beginning of the lesson.	
Step 3: Look at the main part of the lesson.	
Step 4: Read the end of the lesson.	
Question	
One section at a time, change the lesson title, subheads, or bold and highlighted words into *who, what, where, when, why,* or *how* questions.	
Read	
One section at a time, read any question, and write the answer. Reread, and adjust reading rate as needed.	
Reflect	
Step 1: Reread your notes.	
Step 2: Think about how the topic relates to you, your world, and other things you've read.	
Review	
Step 1: Read the questions. Say the answers.	
Step 2: Read the answers. Say the questions.	

Note-Taking Form

Name _____ Date _____

Question (Page Number)	**Answer**

Lesson 3

Word-Learning Strategies

Name _____ Date _____

Word

- -

Context-Clues Strategy

When you come across a word you don't know,

Step 1: Read the sentence containing the word.

Step 2: Look for a definition or for examples of the word in the sentence.

Step 3: Read before or after the sentence for a definition or for examples of the word.

Word Meaning from Context

Glossary Definition

Dictionary Definition

Online-Dictionary Definition

Fluency Practice: Standardized Test

Name _____ Date _____

Isaac Newton, Father of Physical Science

Isaac Newton was one of the most influential figures in the history of science. He invented new mathematical methods. He developed theories about light and color. He wrote laws about mechanics—the study of forces and motion. Much of his work has withstood the test of time. His laws, his theories, and his calculations still hold true.

Early Life and School Days

Newton had a difficult childhood. His father, a farmer, died before Newton was born, and Newton was sent to live with his grandmother when he was three. When he was eleven, he and his mother were reunited, and he left school to work on the farm. From all accounts, he wasn't cut out for farming, so he returned to school.

Newton was an unremarkable student. He didn't begin to realize his full potential until he entered college. At Cambridge University, he studied the teachings of ancient Greek philosophers and mathematicians. On his own, he studied the works of the greatest scientists of his time.

Contributions to Science and Mathematics

After graduation, Newton developed new methods in calculus, a branch of mathematics that plays an important role in physical science. Legend says that during this time Newton observed a falling apple while sitting in an orchard. According to the story, this observation began Newton's study of gravity.

Newton conducted many experiments with light and color. He used prisms to separate white light into the colors of the spectrum. Newton theorized that light travels in straight lines instead of waves. Newton detailed his work in a three-volume work called *Opticks*.

Twenty years of study and experimentation resulted in *Principia*, one of the most important scientific works ever published. Book I details his theories about motion and force, including his three laws of motion. Book II is about the motion of fluids. Book III explains the motion of planets and their moons by the force of gravity. Newton united objects on Earth and in space under one set of laws.

· ·

Score _____ /8 = _____ %

Directions: Take turns reading the questions. Answer the questions together.

Level 1: "Remember" Questions—each worth 1 point

For Level 1 questions, fill in the space next to the correct answer in your own Workbook.

1. Isaac Newton wrote which of the following about mechanics?
   ○ a. Methods
   ○ b. Theories
   ○ c. Books
   ○ d. Laws

Lesson 3

Fluency Practice: Standardized Test, continued

Name _____ Date _____

2. At what age was Newton reunited with his mother?
   ○ a. Three years old   ○ c. Nine years old
   ○ b. Eleven years old   ○ d. Fourteen years old

3. Which subject did Newton study at Cambridge University?
   ○ a. Greek philosphers and mathematicians   ○ c. Farming and agriculture
   ○ b. Astronomy and astrology   ○ d. Writing and literature

4. According to legend, Newton's study of gravity began with which observation?
   ○ a. A rock rolling downhill   ○ c. A falling apple
   ○ b. Falling rain   ○ d. A falling leaf

5. Newton proposed that light
   ○ a. travels in straight lines.   ○ c. travels in waves.
   ○ b. travels through solid objects.   ○ d. travels in circles.

6. How many books are found in the important work *Principia*?
   ○ a. Two   ○ c. Three
   ○ b. Four   ○ d. Five

Level 2: "Understand" Question—worth 2 points (2 points for correct answer, 1 point for partially correct answer, 0 points for incorrect answer)

For the Level 2 question, write the answer in the space provided in your own Workbook.

7. Describe <u>two</u> ways Newton contributed to science and mathematics.

_____

_____

_____

_____

_____

_____

Lesson 4

SQ3R-Strategy Checklist

Name _____ Date _____

	Yes
Survey	

Step 1: Make text connections.
     1: What's the topic of the lesson?
     2: What's your purpose for reading?
     3: What do you know about the topic?	

Step 2: Read the beginning of the lesson.	
Step 3: Look at the main part of the lesson.	
Step 4: Read the end of the lesson.	
Question	
One section at a time, change the lesson title, subheads, or bold and highlighted words into *who, what, where, when, why,* or *how* questions.	
Read	
One section at a time, read any question, and write the answer. Reread, and adjust reading rate as needed.	
Reflect	
Step 1: Reread your notes.	
Step 2: Think about how the topic relates to you, your world, and other things you've read.	
Review	
Step 1: Read the questions. Say the answers.	
Step 2: Read the answers. Say the questions.	

Lesson 4

Note-Taking Form

Name _____ Date _____

Question (Page Number)	Answer

Order-or-Sequence Chart

Name _____ Date _____

```
┌─────────────────────────────────────────┐
│                                         │
└─────────────────────────────────────────┘
                    ↓
┌─────────────────────────────────────────┐
│                                         │
└─────────────────────────────────────────┘
                    ↓
┌─────────────────────────────────────────┐
│                                         │
└─────────────────────────────────────────┘
                    ↓
┌─────────────────────────────────────────┐
│                                         │
└─────────────────────────────────────────┘
                    ↓
┌─────────────────────────────────────────┐
│                                         │
└─────────────────────────────────────────┘
                    ↓
┌─────────────────────────────────────────┐
│                                         │
└─────────────────────────────────────────┘
                    ↓
┌─────────────────────────────────────────┐
│                                         │
└─────────────────────────────────────────┘
                    ↓
┌─────────────────────────────────────────┐
│                                         │
└─────────────────────────────────────────┘
```

Lesson 4

Word-Learning Strategies

Name _____ Date _____

Word

- -

Context-Clues Strategy

When you come across a word you don't know,

Step 1: Read the sentence containing the word.

Step 2: Look for a definition or for examples of the word in the sentence.

Step 3: Read before or after the sentence for a definition or for examples of the word.

Word Meaning from Context

Glossary Definition

Dictionary Definition

Online-Dictionary Definition

Lesson 4

Fluency Practice: Information Learned

Name _____ Date _____

Isaac Newton, Father of Physical Science

Isaac Newton was one of the most influential figures in the history of science. He invented new mathematical methods. He developed theories about light and color. He wrote laws about mechanics—the study of forces and motion. Much of his work has withstood the test of time. His laws, his theories, and his calculations still hold true.

Early Life and School Days

Newton had a difficult childhood. His father, a farmer, died before Newton was born, and Newton was sent to live with his grandmother when he was three. When he was eleven, he and his mother were reunited, and he left school to work on the farm. From all accounts, he wasn't cut out for farming, so he returned to school.

Newton was an unremarkable student. He didn't begin to realize his full potential until he entered college. At Cambridge University, he studied the teachings of ancient Greek philosophers and mathematicians. On his own, he studied the works of the greatest scientists of his time.

Contributions to Science and Mathematics

After graduation, Newton developed new methods in calculus, a branch of mathematics that plays an important role in physical science. Legend says that during this time Newton observed a falling apple while sitting in an orchard. According to the story, this observation began Newton's study of gravity.

Newton conducted many experiments with light and color. He used prisms to separate white light into the colors of the spectrum. Newton theorized that light travels in straight lines instead of waves. Newton detailed his work in a three-volume work called *Opticks*.

Twenty years of study and experimentation resulted in *Principia*, one of the most important scientific works ever published. Book I details his theories about motion and force, including his three laws of motion. Book II is about the motion of fluids. Book III explains the motion of planets and their moons by the force of gravity. Newton united objects on Earth and in space under one set of laws.

Directions: Write three things you learned from reading the fluency passage.

1. I learned _____

_____

2. I learned _____

_____

3. I learned _____

_____

Think-Pair-Share

Name _____ Date _____

Directions

Directions: Use the Think-Pair-Share Strategy to complete the question below.

Step 1: Think about the question for one minute.

Step 2: Pair and complete the question with your partner.

Step 3: Share what you wrote with the class.

Evaluate

Suppose you're a science teacher whose students are learning about Newton's first law of motion. *Evaluate* how well you've taught the concepts of objects in motion and inertia by having your students determine why a snowball rolling downhill may pick up speed and become more difficult to stop.

SQ3R-Strategy Checklist

Name _____ Date _____

	Yes
Survey	

Step 1: Make text connections.
    1: What's the topic of the lesson?
    2: What's your purpose for reading?
    3: What do you know about the topic?	

Step 2: Read the beginning of the lesson.	
Step 3: Look at the main part of the lesson.	
Step 4: Read the end of the lesson.	
Question	
One section at a time, change the lesson title, subheads, or bold and highlighted words into *who, what, where, when, why,* or *how* questions.	
Read	
One section at a time, read any question, and write the answer. Reread, and adjust reading rate as needed.	
Reflect	
Step 1: Reread your notes.	
Step 2: Think about how the topic relates to you, your world, and other things you've read.	
Review	
Step 1: Read the questions. Say the answers.	
Step 2: Read the answers. Say the questions.	

Activity 2

Note-Taking Form

Name _____ Date_____

Question (Page Number)	**Answer**

Word-Learning Strategies

Name _____ Date _____

Word

- -

Context-Clues Strategy

When you come across a word you don't know,

Step 1: Read the sentence containing the word.

↓

Step 2: Look for a definition or for examples of the word in the sentence.

↓

Step 3: Read before or after the sentence for a definition or for examples of the word.

Word Meaning from Context

↓

Glossary Definition

↓

Dictionary Definition

↓

Online-Dictionary Definition

Lesson 2

SQ3R-Strategy Checklist

Name _____ Date _____

	Yes
Survey	
Step 1: Make text connections. **1:** What's the topic of the lesson? **2:** What's your purpose for reading? **3:** What do you know about the topic?	
Step 2: Read the beginning of the lesson.	
Step 3: Look at the main part of the lesson.	
Step 4: Read the end of the lesson.	
Question	
One section at a time, change the lesson title, subheads, or bold and highlighted words into *who, what, where, when, why,* or *how* questions.	
Read	
One section at a time, read any question, and write the answer. Reread, and adjust reading rate as needed.	
Reflect	
Step 1: Reread your notes.	
Step 2: Think about how the topic relates to you, your world, and other things you've read.	
Review	
Step 1: Read the questions. Say the answers.	
Step 2: Read the answers. Say the questions.	

Lesson 2

Note-Taking Form

Name _____ Date _____

Question (Page Number)	**Answer**

Lesson 2

Word-Learning Strategies

Name _____ Date _____

Word

. . . .

Context-Clues Strategy

When you come across a word you don't know,

Step 1: Read the sentence containing the word.

Step 2: Look for a definition or for examples of the word in the sentence.

Step 3: Read before or after the sentence for a definition or for examples of the word.

Word Meaning from Context

Glossary Definition

Dictionary Definition

Online-Dictionary Definition

Lesson 2

Fluency Practice: Decoding Multipart Words

Name _____ Date _____

Hybrid Electric Vehicles: A Cleaner Future

We use electricity every day to operate lights, electronic devices, and other things. Many types of machinery that were once powered only by gasoline can now run on electricity. Cars and trucks are no exception. To decrease petroleum consumption and emissions, many vehicle manufacturers have designed hybrid electric vehicles (HEVs), which are powered by a combination of gasoline and electricity.

Most vehicles run on gasoline. HEVs have two energy sources. One is a gasoline-burning engine. The other is an electric battery. Gasoline is made from oil, a nonrenewable resource. Gasoline produces pollution as it burns. HEVs use less gasoline because some of their power is supplied by electric batteries.

Car manufacturers have devised different ways for vehicles to use this combination of energy sources. Some types of HEVs use gasoline for their primary energy source. These vehicles use the battery-powered electric motor to add power when accelerating. Another type of HEV runs on electricity at lower speeds in the city, but switches to gasoline at higher speeds on the highway. Some models automatically recharge their electric batteries when running on gasoline. During city driving, many HEVs conserve battery power by turning off the motor when the car stops at a traffic light.

Vehicles powered by only electricity must be plugged in to recharge their batteries. HEVs do not need to be plugged in to recharge their electric batteries. The electric battery is recharged by a gas-powered generator. Like their all-gas-powered cousins, HEVs can be refueled at ordinary gas pumps.

The first hybrid electric passenger cars appeared in the United States in 2000. There are many models of HEVs made by several different car manufacturers. There are hybrid electric versions of compact cars, sedans, and sport-utility vehicles. New HEVs cost more than gas-only vehicles. However, HEV owners save money by buying less fuel. Like their gas-powered counterparts, smaller HEVs have greater fuel efficiency than larger vehicles.

Strategy Steps

Step 1: Underline all the vowel sounds.

Step 2: Make a slash between the word parts so each part has one vowel sound.

Step 3: Go back to the beginning of the word, and read the parts in order.

Step 4: Read the whole word.

Word 1

Word 2

Lesson 3

SQ3R-Strategy Checklist

Name _____ Date _____

	Yes
Survey	
Step 1: Make text connections. 1: What's the topic of the lesson? 2: What's your purpose for reading? 3: What do you know about the topic?	
Step 2: Read the beginning of the lesson.	
Step 3: Look at the main part of the lesson.	
Step 4: Read the end of the lesson.	
Question	
One section at a time, change the lesson title, subheads, or bold and highlighted words into *who, what, where, when, why,* or *how* questions.	
Read	
One section at a time, read any question, and write the answer. Reread, and adjust reading rate as needed.	
Reflect	
Step 1: Reread your notes.	
Step 2: Think about how the topic relates to you, your world, and other things you've read.	
Review	
Step 1: Read the questions. Say the answers.	
Step 2: Read the answers. Say the questions.	

Note-Taking Form

Name _____ Date _____

Question (Page Number)	**Answer**

Lesson 3

Word-Learning Strategies

Name _____ Date _____

Word

· ·

Context-Clues Strategy

When you come across a word you don't know,

Step 1: Read the sentence containing the word.

Step 2: Look for a definition or for examples of the word in the sentence.

Step 3: Read before or after the sentence for a definition or for examples of the word.

Word Meaning from Context

Glossary Definition

Dictionary Definition

Online-Dictionary Definition

Lesson 3

Fluency Practice: Standardized Test

Name _____ Date _____

Hybrid Electric Vehicles: A Cleaner Future

We use electricity every day to operate lights, electronic devices, and other things. Many types of machinery that were once powered only by gasoline can now run on electricity. Cars and trucks are no exception. To decrease petroleum consumption and emissions, many vehicle manufacturers have designed hybrid electric vehicles (HEVs), which are powered by a combination of gasoline and electricity.

Most vehicles run on gasoline. HEVs have two energy sources. One is a gasoline-burning engine. The other is an electric battery. Gasoline is made from oil, a nonrenewable resource. Gasoline produces pollution as it burns. HEVs use less gasoline because some of their power is supplied by electric batteries.

Car manufacturers have devised different ways for vehicles to use this combination of energy sources. Some types of HEVs use gasoline for their primary energy source. These vehicles use the battery-powered electric motor to add power when accelerating. Another type of HEV runs on electricity at lower speeds in the city, but switches to gasoline at higher speeds on the highway. Some models automatically recharge their electric batteries when running on gasoline. During city driving, many HEVs conserve battery power by turning off the motor when the car stops at a traffic light.

Vehicles powered by only electricity must be plugged in to recharge their batteries. HEVs do not need to be plugged in to recharge their electric batteries. The electric battery is recharged by a gas-powered generator. Like their all-gas-powered cousins, HEVs can be refueled at ordinary gas pumps.

The first hybrid electric passenger cars appeared in the United States in 2000. There are many models of HEVs made by several different car manufacturers. There are hybrid electric versions of compact cars, sedans, and sport-utility vehicles. New HEVs cost more than gas-only vehicles. However, HEV owners save money by buying less fuel. Like their gas-powered counterparts, smaller HEVs have greater fuel efficiency than larger vehicles.

Score _____ /8 = _____ %

Directions: Take turns reading the questions. Answer the questions together.

Level 1: "Remember" Questions—each worth 1 point

For Level 1 questions, fill in the space next to the correct answer in your own Workbook.

1. HEVs are powered by a combination of gasoline and
   ○ a. electricity.
   ○ b. solar power.
   ○ c. ethanol fuel.
   ○ d. vegetable oil.

Fluency Practice: Standardized Test, continued

Name _____ Date _____

2. What makes HEVs different from most vehicles?
   ○ a. HEVs are heavier.
   ○ b. HEVs have two energy sources.
   ○ c. HEV engines are larger and more powerful.
   ○ d. HEVs can be refueled at gas pumps.

3. At lower speeds in the city, HEVs can switch to
   ○ a. running on gasoline.   ○ c. using gas pumps.
   ○ b. battery power.   ○ d. using kerosene.

4. How do HEVs charge their electric batteries?
   ○ a. HEVs do not need to be charged.
   ○ b. HEVs use a gas-powered generator.
   ○ c. HEVs must be manually cranked every one hundred miles.
   ○ d. HEVs must sit twelve hours before using their batteries again to build energy.

5. In what year did the HEV first make an appearance in the United States?
   ○ a. 2001   ○ c. 1999
   ○ b. 1998   ○ d. 2000

6. How might an HEV owner save money over time?
   ○ a. The owner will buy less gas.
   ○ b. The owner will obtain good insurance rates.
   ○ c. The owner will pay less in licensing fees.
   ○ d. The owner will have fewer car repairs.

Level 2: "Understand" Question—worth 2 points (2 points for correct answer, 1 point for partially correct answer, 0 points for incorrect answer)

For the Level 2 question, write the answer in the space provided in your own Workbook.

7. Describe how HEVs decrease petroleum consumption and emissions.

_____

_____

_____

_____

_____

_____

Lesson 4

SQ3R-Strategy Checklist

Name _____ Date _____

	Yes
Survey	
Step 1: Make text connections. **1:** What's the topic of the lesson? **2:** What's your purpose for reading? **3:** What do you know about the topic?	
Step 2: Read the beginning of the lesson.	
Step 3: Look at the main part of the lesson.	
Step 4: Read the end of the lesson.	
Question	
One section at a time, change the lesson title, subheads, or bold and highlighted words into *who, what, where, when, why,* or *how* questions.	
Read	
One section at a time, read any question, and write the answer. Reread, and adjust reading rate as needed.	
Reflect	
Step 1: Reread your notes.	
Step 2: Think about how the topic relates to you, your world, and other things you've read.	
Review	
Step 1: Read the questions. Say the answers.	
Step 2: Read the answers. Say the questions.	

Unit 12
Science

Activity 2

Lesson 4

Note-Taking Form

Name _____ Date _____

Question (Page Number)	Answer

Lesson 4

Cause-and-Effect Chart

Name _____ Date _____

Cause		Effect
	→	

Cause		Effect
	→	

Cause		Effect
	→	

Lesson 4

Word-Learning Strategies

Name _____ Date _____

Word

• •

Context-Clues Strategy

When you come across a word you don't know,

Step 1: Read the sentence containing the word.

Step 2: Look for a definition or for examples of the word in the sentence.

Step 3: Read before or after the sentence for a definition or for examples of the word.

Word Meaning from Context

Glossary Definition

Dictionary Definition

Online-Dictionary Definition

Fluency Practice: Information Learned

Name _____ Date _____

Hybrid Electric Vehicles: A Cleaner Future

We use electricity every day to operate lights, electronic devices, and other things. Many types of machinery that were once powered only by gasoline can now run on electricity. Cars and trucks are no exception. To decrease petroleum consumption and emissions, many vehicle manufacturers have designed hybrid electric vehicles (HEVs), which are powered by a combination of gasoline and electricity.

Most vehicles run on gasoline. HEVs have two energy sources. One is a gasoline-burning engine. The other is an electric battery. Gasoline is made from oil, a nonrenewable resource. Gasoline produces pollution as it burns. HEVs use less gasoline because some of their power is supplied by electric batteries.

Car manufacturers have devised different ways for vehicles to use this combination of energy sources. Some types of HEVs use gasoline for their primary energy source. These vehicles use the battery-powered electric motor to add power when accelerating. Another type of HEV runs on electricity at lower speeds in the city, but switches to gasoline at higher speeds on the highway. Some models automatically recharge their electric batteries when running on gasoline. During city driving, many HEVs conserve battery power by turning off the motor when the car stops at a traffic light.

Vehicles powered by only electricity must be plugged in to recharge their batteries. HEVs do not need to be plugged in to recharge their electric batteries. The electric battery is recharged by a gas-powered generator. Like their all-gas-powered cousins, HEVs can be refueled at ordinary gas pumps.

The first hybrid electric passenger cars appeared in the United States in 2000. There are many models of HEVs made by several different car manufacturers. There are hybrid electric versions of compact cars, sedans, and sport-utility vehicles. New HEVs cost more than gas-only vehicles. However, HEV owners save money by buying less fuel. Like their gas-powered counterparts, smaller HEVs have greater fuel efficiency than larger vehicles.

Directions: Write three things you learned from reading the fluency passage.

1. I learned _____

_____

2. I learned _____

_____

3. I learned _____

_____

Lesson 5

Think-Pair-Share

Name _____ Date _____

Directions: Use the Think-Pair-Share Strategy to complete the question below.

Step 1: **Think** about the question for one minute.

Step 2: **Pair** and complete the question with your partner.

Step 3: **Share** what you wrote with the class.

Evaluate

Suppose you're listening to your favorite FM radio station, but the station keeps fading in and out. Use your knowledge of signals and electromagnetic waves to *evaluate* possible causes of the problem.

Lesson 1

SQ3R-Strategy Checklist

Name _____ Date _____

	Yes
Survey	

Step 1: Make text connections.
    1: What's the topic of the lesson?
    2: What's your purpose for reading?
    3: What do you know about the topic?	

Step 2: Read the beginning of the lesson.	
Step 3: Look at the main part of the lesson.	
Step 4: Read the end of the lesson.	
Question	
One section at a time, change the lesson title, subheads, or bold and highlighted words into *who, what, where, when, why,* or *how* questions.	
Read	
One section at a time, read any question, and write the answer. Reread, and adjust reading rate as needed.	
Reflect	
Step 1: Reread your notes.	
Step 2: Think about how the topic relates to you, your world, and other things you've read.	
Review	
Step 1: Read the questions. Say the answers.	
Step 2: Read the answers. Say the questions.	

Note-Taking Form

Name _____ Date _____

	Question (Page Number)	Answer

Lesson
1

Word-Learning Strategies

Name _____ Date _____

Word

- -

Context-Clues Strategy

When you come across a word you don't know,

Step 1: Read the sentence containing the word.

Step 2: Look for a definition or for examples of the word in the sentence.

Step 3: Read before or after the sentence for a definition or for examples of the word.

Word Meaning from Context

Glossary Definition

Dictionary Definition

Online-Dictionary Definition

Lesson 2

SQ3R-Strategy Checklist

Name _____ Date _____

	Yes
Survey	
Step 1: Make text connections. **1:** What's the topic of the lesson? **2:** What's your purpose for reading? **3:** What do you know about the topic?	
Step 2: Read the beginning of the lesson.	
Step 3: Look at the main part of the lesson.	
Step 4: Read the end of the lesson.	
Question	
One section at a time, change the lesson title, subheads, or bold and highlighted words into *who, what, where, when, why,* or *how* questions.	
Read	
One section at a time, read any question, and write the answer. Reread, and adjust reading rate as needed.	
Reflect	
Step 1: Reread your notes.	
Step 2: Think about how the topic relates to you, your world, and other things you've read.	
Review	
Step 1: Read the questions. Say the answers.	
Step 2: Read the answers. Say the questions.	

Lesson 2

Note-Taking Form

Name _____ Date _____

Question (Page Number)	Answer

Lesson
2

Word-Learning Strategies

Name _____ Date _____

Word

. . . .

Context-Clues Strategy

When you come across a word you don't know,

Step 1: Read the sentence containing the word.

Step 2: Look for a definition or for examples of the word in the sentence.

Step 3: Read before or after the sentence for a definition or for examples of the word.

Word Meaning from Context

Glossary Definition

Dictionary Definition

Online-Dictionary Definition

Fluency Practice: Decoding Multipart Words

Name _____ Date _____

MRI Scans

The letters *MRI* stand for *magnetic resonance imaging*. MRI allows physicians to "see" inside the body. You've probably heard of X-rays, or perhaps you've even had one. X-rays can show a break in a bone, but they're not useful for showing the soft-tissue parts of the body, such as the brain, the heart, and other soft organs. The pictures or images of soft-tissue parts and bones that MRI produces are accurate and detailed.

MRI uses magnetism, radio waves, and a computer to produce images. A giant magnet surrounds a large tube as long as a human body. The patient lies on a bed that moves into the tube, and the powerful magnet generates a magnetic field. The human body is made up mostly of water, and water is made up of hydrogen and oxygen. The magnetic field of MRI causes the hydrogen protons in the body to line up with the magnetic field. Radio waves transmitted by the MRI scanner cause the protons to absorb energy. Signals from tissues in the body are then relayed to a computer. From the signals, the computer produces an image that can be interpreted by a technician.

MRI is a painless way to check for injury or disease in the human body, and there are no known side effects, so MRI is considered safe. However, there are a few drawbacks. Some patients suffer from claustrophobia, or fear of being in closed or narrow places. Being in the tube may upset them so that they can't lie still for the test. MRI also makes a loud banging noise that some patients find frightening. These patients may be given medication to help them relax.

MRI can be used to check for disease and injury throughout the body. For example, doctors can use MRI to see through the skull to look for brain tumors or bleeding that might indicate a stroke, and MRI can also be used to check the heart for damage from a heart attack.

- -

Strategy Steps

Step 1: Underline all the vowel sounds.

Step 2: Make a slash between the word parts so each part has one vowel sound.

Step 3: Go back to the beginning of the word, and read the parts in order.

Step 4: Read the whole word.

Word 1

Word 2

SQ3R-Strategy Checklist

Name _____ Date _____

	Yes
Survey	
Step 1: Make text connections. 　**1:** What's the topic of the lesson? 　**2:** What's your purpose for reading? 　**3:** What do you know about the topic?	
Step 2: Read the beginning of the lesson.	
Step 3: Look at the main part of the lesson.	
Step 4: Read the end of the lesson.	
Question	
One section at a time, change the lesson title, subheads, or bold and highlighted words into *who, what, where, when, why,* or *how* questions.	
Read	
One section at a time, read any question, and write the answer. Reread, and adjust reading rate as needed.	
Reflect	
Step 1: Reread your notes.	
Step 2: Think about how the topic relates to you, your world, and other things you've read.	
Review	
Step 1: Read the questions. Say the answers.	
Step 2: Read the answers. Say the questions.	

Lesson 3

Note-Taking Form

Name _____ Date _____

Question (Page Number)	**Answer**

Lesson 3

Word-Learning Strategies

Name _____ Date _____

Word

· ·

Context-Clues Strategy

When you come across a word you don't know,

Step 1: Read the sentence containing the word.

Step 2: Look for a definition or for examples of the word in the sentence.

Step 3: Read before or after the sentence for a definition or for examples of the word.

Word Meaning from Context

Glossary Definition

Dictionary Definition

Online-Dictionary Definition

Fluency Practice: Standardized Test

Name _____ Date _____

MRI Scans

The letters *MRI* stand for *magnetic resonance imaging*. MRI allows physicians to "see" inside the body. You've probably heard of X-rays, or perhaps you've even had one. X-rays can show a break in a bone, but they're not useful for showing the soft-tissue parts of the body, such as the brain, the heart, and other soft organs. The pictures or images of soft-tissue parts and bones that MRI produces are accurate and detailed.

MRI uses magnetism, radio waves, and a computer to produce images. A giant magnet surrounds a large tube as long as a human body. The patient lies on a bed that moves into the tube, and the powerful magnet generates a magnetic field. The human body is made up mostly of water, and water is made up of hydrogen and oxygen. The magnetic field of MRI causes the hydrogen protons in the body to line up with the magnetic field. Radio waves transmitted by the MRI scanner cause the protons to absorb energy. Signals from tissues in the body are then relayed to a computer. From the signals, the computer produces an image that can be interpreted by a technician.

MRI is a painless way to check for injury or disease in the human body, and there are no known side effects, so MRI is considered safe. However, there are a few drawbacks. Some patients suffer from claustrophobia, or fear of being in closed or narrow places. Being in the tube may upset them so that they can't lie still for the test. MRI also makes a loud banging noise that some patients find frightening. These patients may be given medication to help them relax.

MRI can be used to check for disease and injury throughout the body. For example, doctors can use MRI to see through the skull to look for brain tumors or bleeding that might indicate a stroke, and MRI can also be used to check the heart for damage from a heart attack.

Score _____ /8 = _____ %

Directions: Take turns reading the questions. Answer the questions together.

Level 1: "Remember" Questions—each worth 1 point

For Level 1 questions, fill in the space next to the correct answer in your own Workbook.

1. What do the letters *MRI* stand for?
   - a. Medical Research Institute
   - b. Magnetic Resonance Imaging
   - c. Major Reconstruction Instrument
   - d. Modern Radioactive Imaging

Lesson

3

Fluency Practice: Standardized Test, continued

Name _____ Date _____

2. MRI allows a doctor to
   - ○ a. see inside the body.
   - ○ b. work on more than one patient at a time.
   - ○ c. perform complex surgeries.
   - ○ d. help patients heal faster.

3. During MRI, the patient lies on a bed that moves into a tube surrounded by a giant
   - ○ a. X-ray machine.
   - ○ b. camera.
   - ○ c. computer.
   - ○ d. magnet.

4. MRI's magnetic field causes the hydrogen in the body to
   - ○ a. bind together.
   - ○ b. light up and show the area or areas with disease or injury.
   - ○ c. line up with the magnetic field.
   - ○ d. speed up the body's healing process.

5. Which of these statements is true about MRI?
   - ○ a. It isn't necessary for patients to lie still during MRI.
   - ○ b. There are a few known side effects from MRI.
   - ○ c. Some patients can suffer from claustrophobia during MRI.
   - ○ d. MRI isn't considered safe.

6. Which one of these people should probably have MRI?
   - ○ a. A young boy who fell and scraped his knee
   - ○ b. A woman who had a heart attack
   - ○ c. A man who bruised his arm
   - ○ d. A teenage boy who burned his hand

Level 2: "Understand" Question—worth 2 points (2 points for correct answer, 1 point for partially correct answer, 0 points for incorrect answer)

For the Level 2 question, write the answer in the space provided in your own Workbook.

7. Explain how MRI works.

_____

_____

_____

_____

_____

_____

SQ3R-Strategy Checklist

Name _____ Date _____

	Yes
Survey	
Step 1: Make text connections. **1:** What's the topic of the lesson? **2:** What's your purpose for reading? **3:** What do you know about the topic?	
Step 2: Read the beginning of the lesson.	
Step 3: Look at the main part of the lesson.	
Step 4: Read the end of the lesson.	
Question	
One section at a time, change the lesson title, subheads, or bold and highlighted words into *who, what, where, when, why,* or *how* questions.	
Read	
One section at a time, read any question, and write the answer. Reread, and adjust reading rate as needed.	
Reflect	
Step 1: Reread your notes.	
Step 2: Think about how the topic relates to you, your world, and other things you've read.	
Review	
Step 1: Read the questions. Say the answers.	
Step 2: Read the answers. Say the questions.	

Lesson 4

Note-Taking Form

Name _____ Date _____

Question (Page Number)	**Answer**

Lesson
4

Compare-and-Contrast Chart

Name _____ Date _____

Different	Same	Different

Lesson 4

Word-Learning Strategies

Name _____ Date _____

Word

....

Context-Clues Strategy

When you come across a word you don't know,

Step 1: Read the sentence containing the word.

Step 2: Look for a definition or for examples of the word in the sentence.

Step 3: Read before or after the sentence for a definition or for examples of the word.

Word Meaning from Context

Glossary Definition

Dictionary Definition

Online-Dictionary Definition

Fluency Practice: Information Learned

Name _____ Date _____

MRI Scans

The letters *MRI* stand for *magnetic resonance imaging*. MRI allows physicians to "see" inside the body. You've probably heard of X-rays, or perhaps you've even had one. X-rays can show a break in a bone, but they're not useful for showing the soft-tissue parts of the body, such as the brain, the heart, and other soft organs. The pictures or images of soft-tissue parts and bones that MRI produces are accurate and detailed.

MRI uses magnetism, radio waves, and a computer to produce images. A giant magnet surrounds a large tube as long as a human body. The patient lies on a bed that moves into the tube, and the powerful magnet generates a magnetic field. The human body is made up mostly of water, and water is made up of hydrogen and oxygen. The magnetic field of MRI causes the hydrogen protons in the body to line up with the magnetic field. Radio waves transmitted by the MRI scanner cause the protons to absorb energy. Signals from tissues in the body are then relayed to a computer. From the signals, the computer produces an image that can be interpreted by a technician.

MRI is a painless way to check for injury or disease in the human body, and there are no known side effects, so MRI is considered safe. However, there are a few drawbacks. Some patients suffer from claustrophobia, or fear of being in closed or narrow places. Being in the tube may upset them so that they can't lie still for the test. MRI also makes a loud banging noise that some patients find frightening. These patients may be given medication to help them relax.

MRI can be used to check for disease and injury throughout the body. For example, doctors can use MRI to see through the skull to look for brain tumors or bleeding that might indicate a stroke, and MRI can also be used to check the heart for damage from a heart attack.

Directions: Write three things you learned from reading the fluency passage.

1. I learned _____

_____

2. I learned _____

_____

3. I learned _____

_____

Lesson 5

Think-Pair-Share

Name _____ Date _____

Evaluate

Suppose you're an artist who has difficulty seeing. Use your knowledge of light and sight to *evaluate* which is more important: the ability to see clearly or the ability to see colors correctly.

Lesson
1

SQ3R-Strategy Checklist

Name _____ Date _____

	Yes
Survey	
Step 1: Make text connections. 　　1: What's the topic of the lesson? 　　2: What's your purpose for reading? 　　3: What do you know about the topic?	
Step 2: Read the beginning of the lesson.	
Step 3: Look at the main part of the lesson.	
Step 4: Read the end of the lesson.	
Question	
One section at a time, change the lesson title, subheads, or bold and highlighted words into *who, what, where, when, why,* or *how* questions.	
Read	
One section at a time, read any question, and write the answer. Reread, and adjust reading rate as needed.	
Reflect	
Step 1: Reread your notes.	
Step 2: Think about how the topic relates to you, your world, and other things you've read.	
Review	
Step 1: Read the questions. Say the answers.	
Step 2: Read the answers. Say the questions.	

Note-Taking Form

Name _____ Date _____

Question (Page Number)	Answer

Lesson

1

Word-Learning Strategies

Name _____ Date _____

Word

⋯⋯⋯⋯⋯⋯⋯⋯⋯⋯⋯⋯⋯⋯⋯⋯⋯⋯⋯⋯⋯⋯⋯⋯⋯⋯⋯⋯⋯

Context-Clues Strategy

When you come across a word you don't know,

Step 1: Read the sentence containing the word.

Step 2: Look for a definition or for examples of the word in the sentence.

Step 3: Read before or after the sentence for a definition or for examples of the word.

Word Meaning from Context

Glossary Definition

Dictionary Definition

Online-Dictionary Definition

Lesson 2

SQ3R-Strategy Checklist

Name _____ Date _____

	Yes
Survey	

Step 1: Make text connections.
    1: What's the topic of the lesson?
    2: What's your purpose for reading?
    3: What do you know about the topic?	

Step 2: Read the beginning of the lesson.	
Step 3: Look at the main part of the lesson.	
Step 4: Read the end of the lesson.	
Question	
One section at a time, change the lesson title, subheads, or bold and highlighted words into *who, what, where, when, why,* or *how* questions.	
Read	
One section at a time, read any question, and write the answer. Reread, and adjust reading rate as needed.	
Reflect	
Step 1: Reread your notes.	
Step 2: Think about how the topic relates to you, your world, and other things you've read.	
Review	
Step 1: Read the questions. Say the answers.	
Step 2: Read the answers. Say the questions.	

Note-Taking Form

Name _____ Date _____

Question (Page Number)	**Answer**

Lesson 2

Word-Learning Strategies

Name _____ Date _____

Word

- -

Context-Clues Strategy

When you come across a word you don't know,

Step 1: Read the sentence containing the word.

Step 2: Look for a definition or for examples of the word in the sentence.

Step 3: Read before or after the sentence for a definition or for examples of the word.

Word Meaning from Context

Glossary Definition

Dictionary Definition

Online-Dictionary Definition

Lesson 2

Fluency Practice: Decoding Multipart Words

Name _____ Date _____

The Lure of the World's Largest Diamonds

A diamond is forever. A person who has many fine qualities but lacks polish is sometimes called a diamond in the rough. There are many sayings about diamonds, but one thing is clear: humans have always wanted diamonds—the bigger, the better. Diamonds are the most sought-after jewel, and the bigger the diamond is, the greater its value can be.

How big is a "big" diamond? The size of diamonds is measured in carats, and a carat is a unit of mass that equals two hundred milligrams. If you consider that the diamond on the average engagement ring in the United States is approximately one-third of a carat, you will understand that most diamonds are fairly small. The largest diamonds in the world are hundreds of carats in size!

Although extremely large diamonds may be impressive, they can be too large for jewelry, and they are sometimes less attractive than smaller diamonds. Diamonds in their natural state don't have the clarity and luster that make them valuable as jewels. A diamond must be cut by an expert to enhance the good material and make it sparkle. A diamond cutter cuts many facets, or faces, on the surface of a diamond, and these facets, cut at different angles, make a diamond sparkle.

The Cullinan diamond holds the record as the largest diamond ever found. It was discovered in South Africa in 1905 and had a mass of more than three thousand carats. It has been cut into hundreds of smaller diamonds. The largest diamond cut from the Cullinan diamond is the Cullinan I, also called the "Star of Africa," which has a mass of 530.2 carats.

One famous diamond, the Hope diamond, is said to be cursed. The Hope diamond is more than forty-five carats and appears slightly blue. It was found in India in the seventeenth century and has been owned by many people, including Marie Antoinette. Legend says that bad luck befalls whoever owns it. You can see the Hope diamond at the Smithsonian Institution in Washington, D.C.

Strategy Steps

Step 1: Underline all the vowel sounds.

Step 2: Make a slash between the word parts so each part has one vowel sound.

Step 3: Go back to the beginning of the word, and read the parts in order.

Step 4: Read the whole word.

Word 1

Word 2

SQ3R-Strategy Checklist

Name _____ Date _____

	Yes
Survey	

Step 1: Make text connections.
    1: What's the topic of the lesson?
    2: What's your purpose for reading?
    3: What do you know about the topic?	

Step 2: Read the beginning of the lesson.	
Step 3: Look at the main part of the lesson.	
Step 4: Read the end of the lesson.	
Question	
One section at a time, change the lesson title, subheads, or bold and highlighted words into *who, what, where, when, why,* or *how* questions.	
Read	
One section at a time, read any question, and write the answer. Reread, and adjust reading rate as needed.	
Reflect	
Step 1: Reread your notes.	
Step 2: Think about how the topic relates to you, your world, and other things you've read.	
Review	
Step 1: Read the questions. Say the answers.	
Step 2: Read the answers. Say the questions.	

Note-Taking Form

Name _____ Date _____

Question (Page Number)	**Answer**

Lesson 3

Word-Learning Strategies

Name _____ Date _____

Word

. . . .

Context-Clues Strategy

When you come across a word you don't know,

Step 1: Read the sentence containing the word.

Step 2: Look for a definition or for examples of the word in the sentence.

Step 3: Read before or after the sentence for a definition or for examples of the word.

Word Meaning from Context

Glossary Definition

Dictionary Definition

Online-Dictionary Definition

Lesson 3

Fluency Practice: Standardized Test

Name _____ Date _____

The Lure of the World's Largest Diamonds

A diamond is forever. A person who has many fine qualities but lacks polish is sometimes called a diamond in the rough. There are many sayings about diamonds, but one thing is clear: humans have always wanted diamonds—the bigger, the better. Diamonds are the most sought-after jewel, and the bigger the diamond is, the greater its value can be.

How big is a "big" diamond? The size of diamonds is measured in carats, and a carat is a unit of mass that equals two hundred milligrams. If you consider that the diamond on the average engagement ring in the United States is approximately one-third of a carat, you will understand that most diamonds are fairly small. The largest diamonds in the world are hundreds of carats in size!

Although extremely large diamonds may be impressive, they can be too large for jewelry, and they are sometimes less attractive than smaller diamonds. Diamonds in their natural state don't have the clarity and luster that make them valuable as jewels. A diamond must be cut by an expert to enhance the good material and make it sparkle. A diamond cutter cuts many facets, or faces, on the surface of a diamond, and these facets, cut at different angles, make a diamond sparkle.

The Cullinan diamond holds the record as the largest diamond ever found. It was discovered in South Africa in 1905 and had a mass of more than three thousand carats. It has been cut into hundreds of smaller diamonds. The largest diamond cut from the Cullinan diamond is the Cullinan I, also called the "Star of Africa," which has a mass of 530.2 carats.

One famous diamond, the Hope diamond, is said to be cursed. The Hope diamond is more than forty-five carats and appears slightly blue. It was found in India in the seventeenth century and has been owned by many people, including Marie Antoinette. Legend says that bad luck befalls whoever owns it. You can see the Hope diamond at the Smithsonian Institution in Washington, D.C.

Score _____ /8 = _____ %

Directions: Take turns reading the questions. Answer the questions together.

Level 1: "Remember" Questions—each worth 1 point

For Level 1 questions, fill in the space next to the correct answer in your own Workbook.

1. The bigger the diamond,
   - ○ a. the more the diamond is worth.
   - ○ b. the more angles the diamond naturally has.
   - ○ c. the better the diamond's color.
   - ○ d. the less people want the diamond.

Lesson
3

Fluency Practice: Standardized Test, continued

Name _____ Date _____

2. How is the size of a diamond measured?
   ○ a. In ounces
   ○ b. In units
   ○ c. In carats
   ○ d. In grams

3. The facets on a diamond are also called
   ○ a. notches.
   ○ b. grooves.
   ○ c. faces.
   ○ d. ruts.

4. How are the facets cut to make the diamond sparkle?
   ○ a. In straight lines
   ○ b. In circles
   ○ c. In spirals
   ○ d. At different angles

5. Where was the Cullinan diamond found?
   ○ a. South Africa
   ○ b. Belize
   ○ c. Spain
   ○ d. Egypt

6. Which of these statements is false about the Hope diamond?
   ○ a. The Hope diamond appears slightly blue.
   ○ b. The Hope diamond is said to be cursed.
   ○ c. The Hope diamond was owned by one person before going to the Smithsonian.
   ○ d. The Hope diamond was found in India.

Level 2: "Understand" Question—worth 2 points (2 points for correct answer, 1 point for partially correct answer, 0 points for incorrect answer)

For the Level 2 question, write the answer in the space provided in your own Workbook.

7. Explain how a diamond gets its clarity and luster.

_____

_____

_____

_____

_____

_____

SQ3R-Strategy Checklist

Name _____ Date _____

	Yes
Survey	
Step 1: Make text connections. 　　1: What's the topic of the lesson? 　　2: What's your purpose for reading? 　　3: What do you know about the topic?	
Step 2: Read the beginning of the lesson.	
Step 3: Look at the main part of the lesson.	
Step 4: Read the end of the lesson.	
Question	
One section at a time, change the lesson title, subheads, or bold and highlighted words into *who, what, where, when, why,* or *how* questions.	
Read	
One section at a time, read any question, and write the answer. Reread, and adjust reading rate as needed.	
Reflect	
Step 1: Reread your notes.	
Step 2: Think about how the topic relates to you, your world, and other things you've read.	
Review	
Step 1: Read the questions. Say the answers.	
Step 2: Read the answers. Say the questions.	

Lesson 4

Note-Taking Form

Name _____ Date _____

Question (Page Number)	Answer

Lesson 4

Description-or-List Chart

Name _____ Date _____

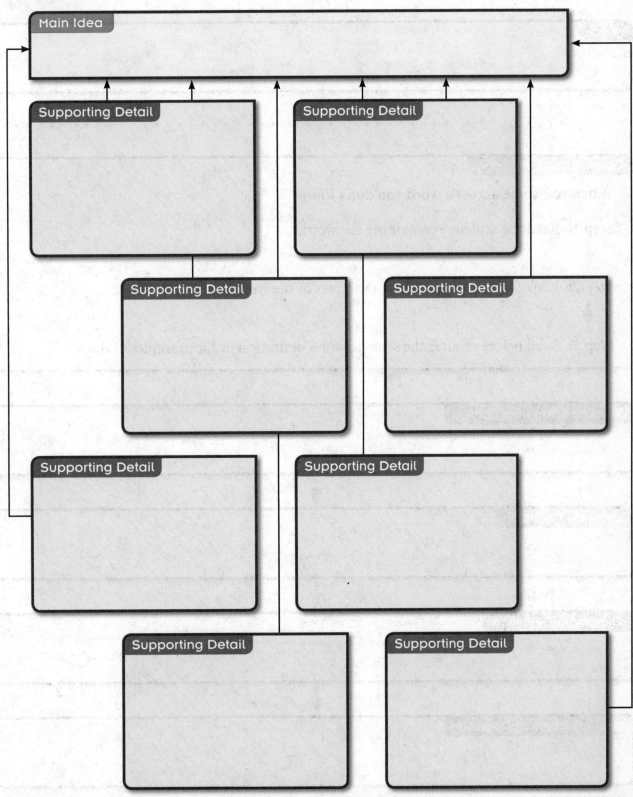

Main Idea

Supporting Detail

Supporting Detail

Supporting Detail

Supporting Detail

Supporting Detail

Supporting Detail

Supporting Detail

Supporting Detail

Lesson **4**

Word-Learning Strategies

Name _____ Date _____

Word

. . . .

Context-Clues Strategy

When you come across a word you don't know,

Step 1: Read the sentence containing the word.

Step 2: Look for a definition or for examples of the word in the sentence.

Step 3: Read before or after the sentence for a definition or for examples of the word.

Word Meaning from Context

Glossary Definition

Dictionary Definition

Online-Dictionary Definition

Lesson 4
Fluency Practice: Information Learned

Name _____ Date _____

The Lure of the World's Largest Diamonds

A diamond is forever. A person who has many fine qualities but lacks polish is sometimes called a diamond in the rough. There are many sayings about diamonds, but one thing is clear: humans have always wanted diamonds—the bigger, the better. Diamonds are the most sought-after jewel, and the bigger the diamond is, the greater its value can be.

How big is a "big" diamond? The size of diamonds is measured in carats, and a carat is a unit of mass that equals two hundred milligrams. If you consider that the diamond on the average engagement ring in the United States is approximately one-third of a carat, you will understand that most diamonds are fairly small. The largest diamonds in the world are hundreds of carats in size!

Although extremely large diamonds may be impressive, they can be too large for jewelry, and they are sometimes less attractive than smaller diamonds. Diamonds in their natural state don't have the clarity and luster that make them valuable as jewels. A diamond must be cut by an expert to enhance the good material and make it sparkle. A diamond cutter cuts many facets, or faces, on the surface of a diamond, and these facets, cut at different angles, make a diamond sparkle.

The Cullinan diamond holds the record as the largest diamond ever found. It was discovered in South Africa in 1905 and had a mass of more than three thousand carats. It has been cut into hundreds of smaller diamonds. The largest diamond cut from the Cullinan diamond is the Cullinan I, also called the "Star of Africa," which has a mass of 530.2 carats.

One famous diamond, the Hope diamond, is said to be cursed. The Hope diamond is more than forty-five carats and appears slightly blue. It was found in India in the seventeenth century and has been owned by many people, including Marie Antoinette. Legend says that bad luck befalls whoever owns it. You can see the Hope diamond at the Smithsonian Institution in Washington, D.C.

Directions: Write three things you learned from reading the fluency passage.

1. I learned _____

_____

2. I learned _____

_____

3. I learned _____

_____

Lesson 5

Think-Pair-Share

Name _____ Date _____

Directions: Use the Think-Pair-Share Strategy to complete the question below.

Step 1: **Think** about the question for one minute.

Step 2: **Pair** and complete the question with your partner.

Step 3: **Share** what you wrote with the class.

Suppose you're a geologist studying land formations in a nearby mountain range when you notice a natural dam has developed in a river bend. *Evaluate* how the processes of the rock cycle will have an impact on the natural dam.

SQ3R/QHL-Strategy Checklist

Name _____ Date _____

SQ3R Strategy	Yes
Survey	

Step 1: Make text connections.
    1: What's the topic of the lesson?
    2: What's your purpose for reading?
    3: What do you know about the topic?	

Step 2: Read the beginning of the lesson.	
Step 3: Look at the main part of the lesson.	
Step 4: Read the end of the lesson.	
Question	
One section at a time, change the lesson title, subheads, or bold and highlighted words into *who, what, where, when, why,* or *how* questions.	
Read	
One section at a time, read any question, and write the answer. Reread, and adjust reading rate as needed.	
Reflect	
Step 1: Reread your notes.	
Step 2: Think about how the topic relates to you, your world, and other things you've read.	
Review	
Step 1: Read the questions. Say the answers.	
Step 2: Read the answers. Say the questions.	
QHL Strategy	
What **Questions** do I have?	
How will I find the answers?	
What did I **Learn** after finding the answers?	

Note-Taking Form

Name _____ Date _____

Question (Page Number)	Answer

Word-Learning Strategies

Name _____ Date _____

Word

· ·

Context-Clues Strategy

When you come across a word you don't know,

Step 1: Read the sentence containing the word.

Step 2: Look for a definition or for examples of the word in the sentence.

Step 3: Read before or after the sentence for a definition or for examples of the word.

Word Meaning from Context

Glossary Definition

Dictionary Definition

Online-Dictionary Definition

Lesson 2

SQ3R/QHL-Strategy Checklist

Name _____ Date _____

SQ3R Strategy	Yes
Survey	
Step 1: Make text connections. **1:** What's the topic of the lesson? **2:** What's your purpose for reading? **3:** What do you know about the topic?	
Step 2: Read the beginning of the lesson.	
Step 3: Look at the main part of the lesson.	
Step 4: Read the end of the lesson.	
Question	
One section at a time, change the lesson title, subheads, or bold and highlighted words into *who, what, where, when, why,* or *how* questions.	
Read	
One section at a time, read any question, and write the answer. Reread, and adjust reading rate as needed.	
Reflect	
Step 1: Reread your notes.	
Step 2: Think about how the topic relates to you, your world, and other things you've read.	
Review	
Step 1: Read the questions. Say the answers.	
Step 2: Read the answers. Say the questions.	
QHL Strategy	
What **Questions** do I have?	
How will I find the answers?	
What did I **Learn** after finding the answers?	

Note-Taking Form

Name _____ Date _____

Question (Page Number)	Answer

Lesson 2

Word-Learning Strategies

Name _____ Date _____

Word

⸳ ⸳

Context-Clues Strategy

When you come across a word you don't know,

Step 1: Read the sentence containing the word.

Step 2: Look for a definition or for examples of the word in the sentence.

Step 3: Read before or after the sentence for a definition or for examples of the word.

Word Meaning from Context

Glossary Definition

Dictionary Definition

Online-Dictionary Definition

Lesson 2

Fluency Practice: Decoding Multipart Words

Name _____ Date _____

The Plant Doctor

George Washington Carver began life in 1864 on a farm near Diamond Grove, Missouri. George had an enslaved mother who worked for the farm's owners, Moses and Susan Carver. Confederate raiders kidnapped George and his mother when the boy was just an infant. Moses Carver rescued George but never found his mother, so the Carvers raised George. As a boy, George collected and studied rocks and plants. The Carvers called him "The Plant Doctor."

At the time, Missouri had separate schools for white and black students, but Diamond Grove had no school for African Americans. At age twelve, George left the farm to go to a one-room school. After completing his early education, George wanted to study science. He traveled from state to state looking for schools that would teach science to an African American. In 1897, Carver received degrees in bacterial biology and agriculture. He became the director of agriculture at the Tuskegee Normal and Industrial Institute for Negroes.

Much of the soil in the South was depleted from decades of growing cotton and tobacco. Cotton and tobacco robbed the soil of nutrients. Carver was determined to help Southern farmers. He used the facilities at the Tuskegee Institute to test ways to enrich soil.

Carver recommended that farmers alternate cotton and tobacco with such crops as peanuts, soybeans, sweet potatoes, and pecans, which enrich the soil. He called this method "crop rotation." Some farmers opposed his ideas because cotton and tobacco had large markets, but demand for the other crops was small.

Carver set out to develop uses for nutrient-rich plants, especially peanuts. Applying his skill as a chemist, he came up with peanut butter, glue, axle grease, bleach, chili sauce, ink, coffee, mayonnaise, metal polish, paper, plastic, pavement, shaving cream, wood stain, artificial rubber, bath powder, and more. Of all these inventions, Carver patented only three. His reason: "God gave them to me. How can I sell them to someone else?"

· ·

Strategy Steps

Step 1: Underline all the vowel sounds.

Step 2: Make a slash between the word parts so each part has one vowel sound.

Step 3: Go back to the beginning of the word, and read the parts in order.

Step 4: Read the whole word.

Word 1

Word 2

SQ3R/QHL-Strategy Checklist

Name _____ Date _____

SQ3R Strategy	Yes
Survey	
Step 1: Make text connections. 1: What's the topic of the lesson? 2: What's your purpose for reading? 3: What do you know about the topic?	
Step 2: Read the beginning of the lesson.	
Step 3: Look at the main part of the lesson.	
Step 4: Read the end of the lesson.	
Question	
One section at a time, change the lesson title, subheads, or bold and highlighted words into *who, what, where, when, why,* or *how* questions.	
Read	
One section at a time, read any question, and write the answer. Reread, and adjust reading rate as needed.	
Reflect	
Step 1: Reread your notes.	
Step 2: Think about how the topic relates to you, your world, and other things you've read.	
Review	
Step 1: Read the questions. Say the answers.	
Step 2: Read the answers. Say the questions.	
QHL Strategy	
What **Questions** do I have?	
How will I find the answers?	
What did I **Learn** after finding the answers?	

Lesson 3

Note-Taking Form

Name _____ Date _____

Question (Page Number)	**Answer**

Lesson 3

Word-Learning Strategies

Name _____ Date _____

Word

- -

Context-Clues Strategy

When you come across a word you don't know,

Step 1: Read the sentence containing the word.

Step 2: Look for a definition or for examples of the word in the sentence.

Step 3: Read before or after the sentence for a definition or for examples of the word.

Word Meaning from Context

Glossary Definition

Dictionary Definition

Online-Dictionary Definition

Lesson 3

Fluency Practice: Standardized Test

Name _____ Date _____

The Plant Doctor

George Washington Carver began life in 1864 on a farm near Diamond Grove, Missouri. George had an enslaved mother who worked for the farm's owners, Moses and Susan Carver. Confederate raiders kidnapped George and his mother when the boy was just an infant. Moses Carver rescued George but never found his mother, so the Carvers raised George. As a boy, George collected and studied rocks and plants. The Carvers called him "The Plant Doctor."

At the time, Missouri had separate schools for white and black students, but Diamond Grove had no school for African Americans. At age twelve, George left the farm to go to a one-room school. After completing his early education, George wanted to study science. He traveled from state to state looking for schools that would teach science to an African American. In 1897, Carver received degrees in bacterial biology and agriculture. He became the director of agriculture at the Tuskegee Normal and Industrial Institute for Negroes.

Much of the soil in the South was depleted from decades of growing cotton and tobacco. Cotton and tobacco robbed the soil of nutrients. Carver was determined to help Southern farmers. He used the facilities at the Tuskegee Institute to test ways to enrich soil.

Carver recommended that farmers alternate cotton and tobacco with such crops as peanuts, soybeans, sweet potatoes, and pecans, which enrich the soil. He called this method "crop rotation." Some farmers opposed his ideas because cotton and tobacco had large markets, but demand for the other crops was small.

Carver set out to develop uses for nutrient-rich plants, especially peanuts. Applying his skill as a chemist, he came up with peanut butter, glue, axle grease, bleach, chili sauce, ink, coffee, mayonnaise, metal polish, paper, plastic, pavement, shaving cream, wood stain, artificial rubber, bath powder, and more. Of all these inventions, Carver patented only three. His reason: "God gave them to me. How can I sell them to someone else?"

- -

Score _____ /8 = _____ %

Directions: Take turns reading the questions. Answer the questions together.

Level 1: "Remember" Questions—each worth 1 point

For Level 1 questions, fill in the space next to the correct answer in your own Workbook.

1. As a young boy, Carver collected and studied
   - ○ a. paper and plastic.
   - ○ b. insects.
   - ○ c. diamonds.
   - ○ d. rocks and plants.

Lesson 3

Fluency Practice: Standardized Test, continued

Name _____ Date _____

2. Carver traveled from state to state,
   ○ a. looking for schools that would teach science to an African American.
   ○ b. learning from well-known scientists and doctors.
   ○ c. collecting and studying insects and plants from each state.
   ○ d. teaching science to young African Americans.

3. In 1897, Carver received degrees in
   ○ a. chemistry and mathematics.
   ○ b. bacterial biology and agriculture.
   ○ c. geology and environmental science.
   ○ d. biology and medicine.

4. Carver wanted to improve the soil that was depleted by growing tobacco and
   ○ a. corn.   ○ c. wheat.
   ○ b. cotton.   ○ d. hay.

5. What was one of the crops Carver recommended as part of the crop-rotation method?
   ○ a. Rice   ○ c. Peanuts
   ○ b. Apples   ○ d. Corn

6. How many inventions did Carver patent?
   ○ a. One   ○ c. Three
   ○ b. Eight   ○ d. Five

Level 2: "Understand" Question—worth 2 points (2 points for correct answer, 1 point for partially correct answer, 0 points for incorrect answer)

For the Level 2 question, write the answer in the space provided in your own Workbook.

7. Explain how crop rotation works.

   _____

   _____

   _____

   _____

   _____

   _____

Lesson 4

SQ3R/QHL-Strategy Checklist

Name _____ Date _____

SQ3R Strategy	Yes
Survey	
Step 1: Make text connections. **1:** What's the topic of the lesson? **2:** What's your purpose for reading? **3:** What do you know about the topic?	
Step 2: Read the beginning of the lesson.	
Step 3: Look at the main part of the lesson.	
Step 4: Read the end of the lesson.	
Question	
One section at a time, change the lesson title, subheads, or bold and highlighted words into *who, what, where, when, why,* or *how* questions.	
Read	
One section at a time, read any question, and write the answer. Reread, and adjust reading rate as needed.	
Reflect	
Step 1: Reread your notes.	
Step 2: Think about how the topic relates to you, your world, and other things you've read.	
Review	
Step 1: Read the questions. Say the answers.	
Step 2: Read the answers. Say the questions.	
QHL Strategy	
What **Questions** do I have?	
How will I find the answers?	
What did I **Learn** after finding the answers?	

Note-Taking Form

Name _____ Date _____

Question (Page Number)	Answer

Order-or-Sequence Chart

Name _____ Date _____

```
┌─────────────────────────────────────────┐
│                                           │
└─────────────────────────────────────────┘
                    ↓
┌─────────────────────────────────────────┐
│                                           │
└─────────────────────────────────────────┘
                    ↓
┌─────────────────────────────────────────┐
│                                           │
└─────────────────────────────────────────┘
                    ↓
┌─────────────────────────────────────────┐
│                                           │
└─────────────────────────────────────────┘
                    ↓
┌─────────────────────────────────────────┐
│                                           │
└─────────────────────────────────────────┘
                    ↓
┌─────────────────────────────────────────┐
│                                           │
└─────────────────────────────────────────┘
                    ↓
┌─────────────────────────────────────────┐
│                                           │
└─────────────────────────────────────────┘
                    ↓
┌─────────────────────────────────────────┐
│                                           │
└─────────────────────────────────────────┘
```

Word-Learning Strategies

Name _____ Date _____

Word

- -

Context-Clues Strategy

When you come across a word you don't know,

Step 1: Read the sentence containing the word.

Step 2: Look for a definition or for examples of the word in the sentence.

Step 3: Read before or after the sentence for a definition or for examples of the word.

Word Meaning from Context

Glossary Definition

Dictionary Definition

Online-Dictionary Definition

Lesson 4

Fluency Practice: Information Learned

Name _____ Date _____

The Plant Doctor

George Washington Carver began life in 1864 on a farm near Diamond Grove, Missouri. George had an enslaved mother who worked for the farm's owners, Moses and Susan Carver. Confederate raiders kidnapped George and his mother when the boy was just an infant. Moses Carver rescued George but never found his mother, so the Carvers raised George. As a boy, George collected and studied rocks and plants. The Carvers called him "The Plant Doctor."

At the time, Missouri had separate schools for white and black students, but Diamond Grove had no school for African Americans. At age twelve, George left the farm to go to a one-room school. After completing his early education, George wanted to study science. He traveled from state to state looking for schools that would teach science to an African American. In 1897, Carver received degrees in bacterial biology and agriculture. He became the director of agriculture at the Tuskegee Normal and Industrial Institute for Negroes.

Much of the soil in the South was depleted from decades of growing cotton and tobacco. Cotton and tobacco robbed the soil of nutrients. Carver was determined to help Southern farmers. He used the facilities at the Tuskegee Institute to test ways to enrich soil.

Carver recommended that farmers alternate cotton and tobacco with such crops as peanuts, soybeans, sweet potatoes, and pecans, which enrich the soil. He called this method "crop rotation." Some farmers opposed his ideas because cotton and tobacco had large markets, but demand for the other crops was small.

Carver set out to develop uses for nutrient-rich plants, especially peanuts. Applying his skill as a chemist, he came up with peanut butter, glue, axle grease, bleach, chili sauce, ink, coffee, mayonnaise, metal polish, paper, plastic, pavement, shaving cream, wood stain, artificial rubber, bath powder, and more. Of all these inventions, Carver patented only three. His reason: "God gave them to me. How can I sell them to someone else?"

- -

Directions: Write three things you learned from reading the fluency passage.

1. I learned _____

_____

2. I learned _____

_____

3. I learned _____

_____

Lesson 5

Think-Pair-Share

Name _____ Date _____

Directions

Directions: Use the Think-Pair-Share Strategy to complete the question below.

Step 1: **Think** about the question for one minute.

Step 2: **Pair** and complete the question with your partner.

Step 3: **Share** what you wrote with the class.

. . . .

Evaluate

Suppose you're a pioneer traveling westward with your family to settle on new land. You have very little room in your wagon for supplies. *Evaluate* what supplies will be the most important on your journey.

SQ3R/QHL-Strategy Checklist

Name _____ Date _____

SQ3R Strategy	Yes
Survey	

Step 1: Make text connections.
    1: What's the topic of the lesson?
    2: What's your purpose for reading?
    3: What do you know about the topic?	

Step 2: Read the beginning of the lesson.	
Step 3: Look at the main part of the lesson.	
Step 4: Read the end of the lesson.	
Question	
One section at a time, change the lesson title, subheads, or bold and highlighted words into *who, what, where, when, why,* or *how* questions.	
Read	
One section at a time, read any question, and write the answer. Reread, and adjust reading rate as needed.	
Reflect	
Step 1: Reread your notes.	
Step 2: Think about how the topic relates to you, your world, and other things you've read.	
Review	
Step 1: Read the questions. Say the answers.	
Step 2: Read the answers. Say the questions.	
QHL Strategy	
What **Questions** do I have?	
How will I find the answers?	
What did I **Learn** after finding the answers?	

Note-Taking Form

Name _____ Date _____

Question (Page Number)	Answer

Word-Learning Strategies

Name _____ Date _____

Word

Context-Clues Strategy

When you come across a word you don't know,

Step 1: Read the sentence containing the word.

Step 2: Look for a definition or for examples of the word in the sentence.

Step 3: Read before or after the sentence for a definition or for examples of the word.

Word Meaning from Context

Glossary Definition

Dictionary Definition

Online-Dictionary Definition

Lesson 2

SQ3R/QHL-Strategy Checklist

Name _____ Date _____

SQ3R Strategy	Yes
Survey	
Step 1: Make text connections. **1:** What's the topic of the lesson? **2:** What's your purpose for reading? **3:** What do you know about the topic?	
Step 2: Read the beginning of the lesson.	
Step 3: Look at the main part of the lesson.	
Step 4: Read the end of the lesson.	
Question	
One section at a time, change the lesson title, subheads, or bold and highlighted words into *who, what, where, when, why,* or *how* questions.	
Read	
One section at a time, read any question, and write the answer. Reread, and adjust reading rate as needed.	
Reflect	
Step 1: Reread your notes.	
Step 2: Think about how the topic relates to you, your world, and other things you've read.	
Review	
Step 1: Read the questions. Say the answers.	
Step 2: Read the answers. Say the questions.	
QHL Strategy	
What **Questions** do I have?	
How will I find the answers?	
What did I **Learn** after finding the answers?	

Lesson
2

Note-Taking Form

Name _____ Date _____

Question (Page Number)	**Answer**

Lesson **2**

Word-Learning Strategies

Name _____ Date _____

Word

· ·

Context-Clues Strategy

When you come across a word you don't know,

Step 1: Read the sentence containing the word.

Step 2: Look for a definition or for examples of the word in the sentence.

Step 3: Read before or after the sentence for a definition or for examples of the word.

Word Meaning from Context

Glossary Definition

Dictionary Definition

Online-Dictionary Definition

Lesson 2

Fluency Practice: Decoding Multipart Words

Name _____ Date _____

Buffalo and the Iron Horse

In the mid-nineteenth century, Cheyenne, Arapaho, Sioux, and dozens of other Native American groups lived on the Great Plains. The millions of buffalo roaming the plains sustained these people's way of life. American Indians ate buffalo meat, fueled their fires with buffalo chips, made glue from buffalo hooves, and covered their tepees with buffalo hides. The buffalo filled almost all their needs.

Despite the presence of Indians and buffalo, American businesspeople considered the Great Plains empty. They planned to bridge the gap between eastern cities and Pacific ports with a transcontinental railroad. In 1862, Congress gave railroad companies funds and granted them thousands of acres to lay their tracks. With the promise of cheap land, railroad officials enticed Easterners to move west and build towns along the future route of the rails.

Before the Civil War ended, the government set up army posts on the plains to protect townspeople and railroad workers. The posts hired hunters, such as "Buffalo Bill" Cody, to provide buffalo meat for the soldiers. The buffalo hunters also supplied meat to thousands of workers. Buffalo Bill alone killed 4,128 buffalo in a year and a half. Other hunters averaged 150 kills a day.

When the first locomotives chugged through the plains, Native Americans called them "iron horses." A herd of buffalo could stall an iron horse for half a day as the herd crossed the tracks. The railroad companies decided to solve this problem by inviting sportsmen to hunt by rail. Hunters shot thousands of buffalo from the trains, often leaving the carcasses behind.

By the late 1870s, only about two thousand buffalo remained in the United States. In just fifteen years, the Plains Indians' way of life had vanished. Native Americans responded by raiding white settlements for food and other necessities. The army retaliated by burning Indian villages. Eventually, Native Americans had little choice but to settle on reservations and live off handouts from the government.

Strategy Steps

Step 1: Underline all the vowel sounds.

Step 2: Make a slash between the word parts so each part has one vowel sound.

Step 3: Go back to the beginning of the word, and read the parts in order.

Step 4: Read the whole word.

Word 1

Word 2

Lesson 3

SQ3R/QHL-Strategy Checklist

Name _____ Date _____

SQ3R Strategy	Yes
Survey	
Step 1: Make text connections. 1: What's the topic of the lesson? 2: What's your purpose for reading? 3: What do you know about the topic?	
Step 2: Read the beginning of the lesson.	
Step 3: Look at the main part of the lesson.	
Step 4: Read the end of the lesson.	
Question	
One section at a time, change the lesson title, subheads, or bold and highlighted words into *who, what, where, when, why,* or *how* questions.	
Read	
One section at a time, read any question, and write the answer. Reread, and adjust reading rate as needed.	
Reflect	
Step 1: Reread your notes.	
Step 2: Think about how the topic relates to you, your world, and other things you've read.	
Review	
Step 1: Read the questions. Say the answers.	
Step 2: Read the answers. Say the questions.	
QHL Strategy	
What **Questions** do I have?	
How will I find the answers?	
What did I **Learn** after finding the answers?	

Note-Taking Form

Name _____ Date _____

Question (Page Number)	**Answer**

Lesson
3

Word-Learning Strategies

Name _____ Date _____

Word

Context-Clues Strategy

When you come across a word you don't know,

Step 1: Read the sentence containing the word.

Step 2: Look for a definition or for examples of the word in the sentence.

Step 3: Read before or after the sentence for a definition or for examples of the word.

Word Meaning from Context

Glossary Definition

Dictionary Definition

Online-Dictionary Definition

Fluency Practice: Standardized Test

Name _____ Date _____

Buffalo and the Iron Horse

In the mid-nineteenth century, Cheyenne, Arapaho, Sioux, and dozens of other Native American groups lived on the Great Plains. The millions of buffalo roaming the plains sustained these people's way of life. American Indians ate buffalo meat, fueled their fires with buffalo chips, made glue from buffalo hooves, and covered their tepees with buffalo hides. The buffalo filled almost all their needs.

Despite the presence of Indians and buffalo, American businesspeople considered the Great Plains empty. They planned to bridge the gap between eastern cities and Pacific ports with a transcontinental railroad. In 1862, Congress gave railroad companies funds and granted them thousands of acres to lay their tracks. With the promise of cheap land, railroad officials enticed Easterners to move west and build towns along the future route of the rails.

Before the Civil War ended, the government set up army posts on the plains to protect townspeople and railroad workers. The posts hired hunters, such as "Buffalo Bill" Cody, to provide buffalo meat for the soldiers. The buffalo hunters also supplied meat to thousands of workers. Buffalo Bill alone killed 4,128 buffalo in a year and a half. Other hunters averaged 150 kills a day.

When the first locomotives chugged through the plains, Native Americans called them "iron horses." A herd of buffalo could stall an iron horse for half a day as the herd crossed the tracks. The railroad companies decided to solve this problem by inviting sportsmen to hunt by rail. Hunters shot thousands of buffalo from the trains, often leaving the carcasses behind.

By the late 1870s, only about two thousand buffalo remained in the United States. In just fifteen years, the Plains Indians' way of life had vanished. Native Americans responded by raiding white settlements for food and other necessities. The army retaliated by burning Indian villages. Eventually, Native Americans had little choice but to settle on reservations and live off handouts from the government.

Score _____ /8 = _____ %

Directions: Take turns reading the questions. Answer the questions together.

Level 1: "Remember" Questions—each worth 1 point

For Level 1 questions, fill in the space next to the correct answer in your own Workbook.

1. Native Americans called the early locomotives
   - ○ a. monsters.
   - ○ b. thunder.
   - ○ c. iron horses.
   - ○ d. steel buffalo.

Lesson 3

Fluency Practice: Standardized Test, continued

Name _____ Date _____

2. Which of the following was planned to bridge the gap between Eastern cities and Pacific ports?
   ○ a. Telephone service
   ○ b. Better wagon trails
   ○ c. The postal service
   ○ d. The transcontinental railroad

3. To entice Easterners to move west and build towns along the way, officials used the promise of
   ○ a. cheap land.
   ○ b. no taxes.
   ○ c. finding gold.
   ○ d. government subsidies.

4. Who was hired to provide buffalo meat for the soldiers on the plains?
   ○ a. The Cheyenne Indians
   ○ b. "Buffalo Bill" Cody
   ○ c. Billy the Kid
   ○ d. Chief Sitting Bull.

5. By the late 1870s, about how many buffalo remained in the United States?
   ○ a. Six thousand
   ○ b. One thousand
   ○ c. Four thousand
   ○ d. Two thousand

6. Where did most of the Plains Indians eventually have to settle?
   ○ a. In Native American villages
   ○ b. On reservations
   ○ c. In white settlements
   ○ d. In big cities

Level 2: "Understand" Question—worth 2 points (2 points for correct answer, 1 point for partially correct answer, 0 points for incorrect answer)

For the Level 2 question, write the answer in the space provided in your own Workbook.

7. Explain how in fifteen years the Plains Indians' way of life vanished.

_____

_____

_____

_____

_____

_____

Lesson 4

SQ3R/QHL-Strategy Checklist

Name _____ Date _____

SQ3R Strategy	Yes
Survey	
Step 1: Make text connections. 1: What's the topic of the lesson? 2: What's your purpose for reading? 3: What do you know about the topic?	
Step 2: Read the beginning of the lesson.	
Step 3: Look at the main part of the lesson.	
Step 4: Read the end of the lesson.	
Question	
One section at a time, change the lesson title, subheads, or bold and highlighted words into *who, what, where, when, why,* or *how* questions.	
Read	
One section at a time, read any question, and write the answer. Reread, and adjust reading rate as needed.	
Reflect	
Step 1: Reread your notes.	
Step 2: Think about how the topic relates to you, your world, and other things you've read.	
Review	
Step 1: Read the questions. Say the answers.	
Step 2: Read the answers. Say the questions.	
QHL Strategy	
What **Questions** do I have?	
How will I find the answers?	
What did I **Learn** after finding the answers?	

Lesson 4

Note-Taking Form

Name _____ Date _____

Question (Page Number)	**Answer**

Lesson 4

Cause-and-Effect Chart

Name _____ Date _____

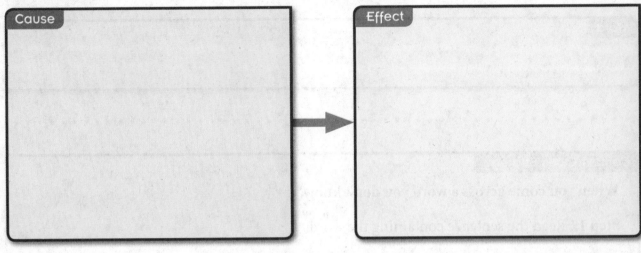

Cause

Effect

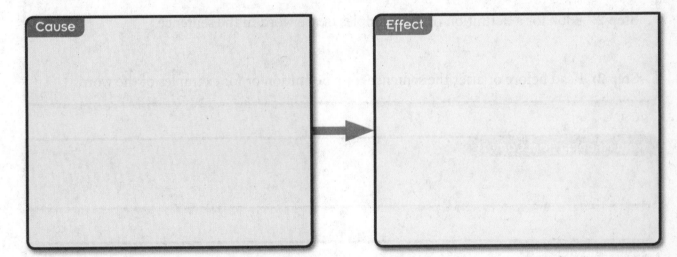

Cause

Effect

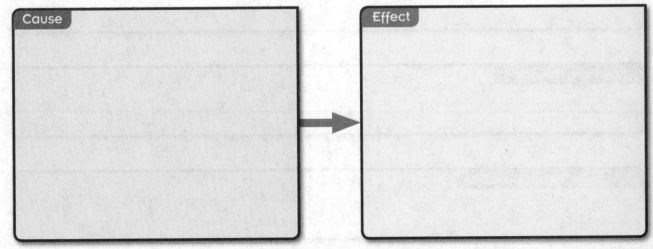

Cause

Effect

Lesson 4

Word-Learning Strategies

Name _____ Date _____

Word

· ·

Context-Clues Strategy

When you come across a word you don't know,

Step 1: Read the sentence containing the word.

Step 2: Look for a definition or for examples of the word in the sentence.

Step 3: Read before or after the sentence for a definition or for examples of the word.

Word Meaning from Context

Glossary Definition

Dictionary Definition

Online-Dictionary Definition

Lesson 4

Fluency Practice: Information Learned

Name _____ Date _____

Buffalo and the Iron Horse

In the mid-nineteenth century, Cheyenne, Arapaho, Sioux, and dozens of other Native American groups lived on the Great Plains. The millions of buffalo roaming the plains sustained these people's way of life. American Indians ate buffalo meat, fueled their fires with buffalo chips, made glue from buffalo hooves, and covered their tepees with buffalo hides. The buffalo filled almost all their needs.

Despite the presence of Indians and buffalo, American businesspeople considered the Great Plains empty. They planned to bridge the gap between eastern cities and Pacific ports with a transcontinental railroad. In 1862, Congress gave railroad companies funds and granted them thousands of acres to lay their tracks. With the promise of cheap land, railroad officials enticed Easterners to move west and build towns along the future route of the rails.

Before the Civil War ended, the government set up army posts on the plains to protect townspeople and railroad workers. The posts hired hunters, such as "Buffalo Bill" Cody, to provide buffalo meat for the soldiers. The buffalo hunters also supplied meat to thousands of workers. Buffalo Bill alone killed 4,128 buffalo in a year and a half. Other hunters averaged 150 kills a day.

When the first locomotives chugged through the plains, Native Americans called them "iron horses." A herd of buffalo could stall an iron horse for half a day as the herd crossed the tracks. The railroad companies decided to solve this problem by inviting sportsmen to hunt by rail. Hunters shot thousands of buffalo from the trains, often leaving the carcasses behind.

By the late 1870s, only about two thousand buffalo remained in the United States. In just fifteen years, the Plains Indians' way of life had vanished. Native Americans responded by raiding white settlements for food and other necessities. The army retaliated by burning Indian villages. Eventually, Native Americans had little choice but to settle on reservations and live off handouts from the government.

Directions: Write three things you learned from reading the fluency passage.

1. I learned _____

_____

2. I learned _____

_____

3. I learned _____

_____

Lesson 5

Think-Pair-Share

Name _____ Date _____

Directions

Directions: Use the Think-Pair-Share Strategy to complete the question below.

Step 1: **Think** about the question for one minute.

Step 2: **Pair** and complete the question with your partner.

Step 3: **Share** what you wrote with the class.

Create

Suppose an adult thinks a type of music or music artist you really like is inappropriate. Use your knowledge of the similarities and differences between your current situation and the 1950s situation with Elvis Presley to *create* a short play showing both your side and the adult's side of the issue.

SQ3R/QHL-Strategy Checklist

Name _____ Date _____

SQ3R Strategy	Yes
Survey	

Step 1: Make text connections.
    1: What's the topic of the lesson?
    2: What's your purpose for reading?
    3: What do you know about the topic?	

Step 2: Read the beginning of the lesson.	
Step 3: Look at the main part of the lesson.	
Step 4: Read the end of the lesson.	
Question	
One section at a time, change the lesson title, subheads, or bold and highlighted words into *who, what, where, when, why,* or *how* questions.	
Read	
One section at a time, read any question, and write the answer. Reread, and adjust reading rate as needed.	
Reflect	
Step 1: Reread your notes.	
Step 2: Think about how the topic relates to you, your world, and other things you've read.	
Review	
Step 1: Read the questions. Say the answers.	
Step 2: Read the answers. Say the questions.	
QHL Strategy	
What **Questions** do I have?	
How will I find the answers?	
What did I **Learn** after finding the answers?	

Note-Taking Form

Name _____ Date _____

Question (Page Number)	Answer

Word-Learning Strategies

Name _____ Date _____

Word

. . . .

Context-Clues Strategy

When you come across a word you don't know,

Step 1: Read the sentence containing the word.

↓

Step 2: Look for a definition or for examples of the word in the sentence.

↓

Step 3: Read before or after the sentence for a definition or for examples of the word.

Word Meaning from Context

↓

Glossary Definition

↓

Dictionary Definition

↓

Online-Dictionary Definition

SQ3R/QHL-Strategy Checklist

Name _____ Date _____

SQ3R Strategy	Yes
Survey	

Step 1: Make text connections.
    1: What's the topic of the lesson?
    2: What's your purpose for reading?
    3: What do you know about the topic?	

Step 2: Read the beginning of the lesson.	
Step 3: Look at the main part of the lesson.	
Step 4: Read the end of the lesson.	
Question	
One section at a time, change the lesson title, subheads, or bold and highlighted words into *who, what, where, when, why,* or *how* questions.	
Read	
One section at a time, read any question, and write the answer. Reread, and adjust reading rate as needed.	
Reflect	
Step 1: Reread your notes.	
Step 2: Think about how the topic relates to you, your world, and other things you've read.	
Review	
Step 1: Read the questions. Say the answers.	
Step 2: Read the answers. Say the questions.	
QHL Strategy	
What **Q**uestions do I have?	
How will I find the answers?	
What did I **L**earn after finding the answers?	

Lesson 2

Note-Taking Form

Name _____ Date _____

Question (Page Number)	Answer

Lesson
2

Word-Learning Strategies

Name _____ Date _____

Word

· ·

Context-Clues Strategy

When you come across a word you don't know,

Step 1: Read the sentence containing the word.

Step 2: Look for a definition or for examples of the word in the sentence.

Step 3: Read before or after the sentence for a definition or for examples of the word.

Word Meaning from Context

Glossary Definition

Dictionary Definition

Online-Dictionary Definition

Fluency Practice: Decoding Multipart Words

Name _____ Date _____

Geologists—History's Detectives

Ask people what they think a geologist does, and chances are most will respond that a geologist collects or examines rocks. Although rocks are at the core of the science of geology, geologists have a variety of roles, many of which might surprise you. One role geologists play is that of history detective.

Rocks are some of the tools we use to learn about Earth's history. Geologists are the experts who can help determine the ages of structures and fossils. Often this information can solve perplexing mysteries about Earth's past.

One such mystery is the disappearance of the dinosaurs. Scientists had known about dinosaurs for a long time. They had evidence of the lives and development of dinosaurs through millions of years. By examining fossils, they learned that dinosaurs disappeared rather suddenly. What caused this disappearance? Scientists developed several theories.

The work of geologists helped provide most of the information to solve the mystery. Many scientists determined that dinosaurs had become extinct approximately sixty-five million years ago. Geologists examined rocks that were sixty-five million years old and found that these rocks contained traces of the metal iridium. This metal is generally scarce but is frequently found in rock layers that are sixty-five million years old. Scientists knew that many asteroids contain iridium. After putting together the pieces provided by geologists, most scientists came to believe that an asteroid had struck Earth sixty-five million years ago, kicking up huge clouds of dust that blocked the sun, which caused plant life on Earth to die, and thus caused dinosaurs to become extinct.

Another way geologists act as detectives is by finding oil and other fossil fuels. Without the skills of geologists, humans might never find the elusive deposits of oil that exist deep underground. Geologists take samples of rocks in several locations and examine them. They use their knowledge of how oil and rocks form to propose theories about the history of a location. They then narrow the possible locations to determine the best spots to drill.

Strategy Steps

Step 1: Underline all the vowel sounds.

Step 2: Make a slash between the word parts so each part has one vowel sound.

Step 3: Go back to the beginning of the word, and read the parts in order.

Step 4: Read the whole word.

Word 1

Word 2

Lesson
3

SQ3R/QHL-Strategy Checklist

Name _____ Date _____

SQ3R Strategy	Yes
Survey	
Step 1: Make text connections. 1: What's the topic of the lesson? 2: What's your purpose for reading? 3: What do you know about the topic?	
Step 2: Read the beginning of the lesson.	
Step 3: Look at the main part of the lesson.	
Step 4: Read the end of the lesson.	
Question	
One section at a time, change the lesson title, subheads, or bold and highlighted words into *who, what, where, when, why,* or *how* questions.	
Read	
One section at a time, read any question, and write the answer. Reread, and adjust reading rate as needed.	
Reflect	
Step 1: Reread your notes.	
Step 2: Think about how the topic relates to you, your world, and other things you've read.	
Review	
Step 1: Read the questions. Say the answers.	
Step 2: Read the answers. Say the questions.	
QHL Strategy	
What **Questions** do I have?	
How will I find the answers?	
What did I **Learn** after finding the answers?	

Lesson 3

Note-Taking Form

Name _____ Date _____

Question (Page Number)	Answer

Lesson 3

Word-Learning Strategies

Name _____ Date _____

Word

- -

Context-Clues Strategy

When you come across a word you don't know,

Step 1: Read the sentence containing the word.

Step 2: Look for a definition or for examples of the word in the sentence.

Step 3: Read before or after the sentence for a definition or for examples of the word.

Word Meaning from Context

Glossary Definition

Dictionary Definition

Online-Dictionary Definition

Lesson 3

Fluency Practice: Standardized Test

Name _____ Date _____

Geologists—History's Detectives

Ask people what they think a geologist does, and chances are most will respond that a geologist collects or examines rocks. Although rocks are at the core of the science of geology, geologists have a variety of roles, many of which might surprise you. One role geologists play is that of history detective.

Rocks are some of the tools we use to learn about Earth's history. Geologists are the experts who can help determine the ages of structures and fossils. Often this information can solve perplexing mysteries about Earth's past.

One such mystery is the disappearance of the dinosaurs. Scientists had known about dinosaurs for a long time. They had evidence of the lives and development of dinosaurs through millions of years. By examining fossils, they learned that dinosaurs disappeared rather suddenly. What caused this disappearance? Scientists developed several theories.

The work of geologists helped provide most of the information to solve the mystery. Many scientists determined that dinosaurs had become extinct approximately sixty-five million years ago. Geologists examined rocks that were sixty-five million years old and found that these rocks contained traces of the metal iridium. This metal is generally scarce but is frequently found in rock layers that are sixty-five million years old. Scientists knew that many asteroids contain iridium. After putting together the pieces provided by geologists, most scientists came to believe that an asteroid had struck Earth sixty-five million years ago, kicking up huge clouds of dust that blocked the sun, which caused plant life on Earth to die, and thus caused dinosaurs to become extinct.

Another way geologists act as detectives is by finding oil and other fossil fuels. Without the skills of geologists, humans might never find the elusive deposits of oil that exist deep underground. Geologists take samples of rocks in several locations and examine them. They use their knowledge of how oil and rocks form to propose theories about the history of a location. They then narrow the possible locations to determine the best spots to drill.

Score _____ /8 = _____ %

Directions: Take turns reading the questions. Answer the questions together.

| **Level 1:** "Remember" Questions—each worth 1 point |

For Level 1 questions, fill in the space next to the correct answer in your own Workbook.

1. A surprising role geologists play is
   - ○ a. history detective.
   - ○ b. environmentalist.
   - ○ c. teacher.
   - ○ d. biologist.

Fluency Practice: Standardized Test, continued

Name _____ Date _____

2. Geologists are the experts who help determine

- ○ a. what ancient cultures were like.
- ○ b. the ages of structures and fossils.
- ○ c. whether plants are native to a particular area.
- ○ d. types of life found in certain regions.

3. Scientists learned that dinosaurs disappeared suddenly by examining

- ○ a. plant samples.
- ○ c. hieroglyphics.
- ○ b. fossils.
- ○ d. Earth's mantle.

4. Many scientists determined that dinosaurs became extinct approximately

- ○ a. sixty-five thousand years ago.
- ○ b. seventy-five million years ago.
- ○ c. sixty-five million years ago.
- ○ d. twenty-five thousand years ago.

5. Traces of which metal may be found in rocks once hit by an asteroid?

- ○ a. Iridium
- ○ c. Gold
- ○ b. Platinum
- ○ d. Copper

6. A second way geologists act as detectives is by helping to find

- ○ a. better ways to grow crops.
- ○ b. lost cities and their treasures.
- ○ c. old growth timber in forests.
- ○ d. oil deposits.

Level 2: "Understand" Question—worth 2 points (2 points for correct answer, 1 point for partially correct answer, 0 points for incorrect answer)

For the Level 2 question, write the answer in the space provided in your own Workbook.

7. Explain how geologists helped solve the mystery of the dinosaurs' disappearance.

_____

_____

_____

_____

_____

_____

SQ3R/QHL-Strategy Checklist

Name _____ Date _____

SQ3R Strategy	Yes
Survey	
Step 1: Make text connections. 　　　1: What's the topic of the lesson? 　　　2: What's your purpose for reading? 　　　3: What do you know about the topic?	
Step 2: Read the beginning of the lesson.	
Step 3: Look at the main part of the lesson.	
Step 4: Read the end of the lesson.	
Question	
One section at a time, change the lesson title, subheads, or bold and highlighted words into *who, what, where, when, why,* or *how* questions.	
Read	
One section at a time, read any question, and write the answer. Reread, and adjust reading rate as needed.	
Reflect	
Step 1: Reread your notes.	
Step 2: Think about how the topic relates to you, your world, and other things you've read.	
Review	
Step 1: Read the questions. Say the answers.	
Step 2: Read the answers. Say the questions.	
QHL Strategy	
What **Questions** do I have?	
How will I find the answers?	
What did I **Learn** after finding the answers?	

Lesson 4

Note-Taking Form

Name _____ Date _____

Question (Page Number)	**Answer**

Compare-and-Contrast Chart

Name _____ Date _____

Different	Same	Different

Word-Learning Strategies

Name _____ Date _____

Word

· ·

Context-Clues Strategy

When you come across a word you don't know,

Step 1: Read the sentence containing the word.

Step 2: Look for a definition or for examples of the word in the sentence.

Step 3: Read before or after the sentence for a definition or for examples of the word.

Word Meaning from Context

Glossary Definition

Dictionary Definition

Online-Dictionary Definition

Lesson 4

Fluency Practice: Information Learned

Name _____ Date _____

Geologists—History's Detectives

Ask people what they think a geologist does, and chances are most will respond that a geologist collects or examines rocks. Although rocks are at the core of the science of geology, geologists have a variety of roles, many of which might surprise you. One role geologists play is that of history detective.

Rocks are some of the tools we use to learn about Earth's history. Geologists are the experts who can help determine the ages of structures and fossils. Often this information can solve perplexing mysteries about Earth's past.

One such mystery is the disappearance of the dinosaurs. Scientists had known about dinosaurs for a long time. They had evidence of the lives and development of dinosaurs through millions of years. By examining fossils, they learned that dinosaurs disappeared rather suddenly. What caused this disappearance? Scientists developed several theories.

The work of geologists helped provide most of the information to solve the mystery. Many scientists determined that dinosaurs had become extinct approximately sixty-five million years ago. Geologists examined rocks that were sixty-five million years old and found that these rocks contained traces of the metal iridium. This metal is generally scarce but is frequently found in rock layers that are sixty-five million years old. Scientists knew that many asteroids contain iridium. After putting together the pieces provided by geologists, most scientists came to believe that an asteroid had struck Earth sixty-five million years ago, kicking up huge clouds of dust that blocked the sun, which caused plant life on Earth to die, and thus caused dinosaurs to become extinct.

Another way geologists act as detectives is by finding oil and other fossil fuels. Without the skills of geologists, humans might never find the elusive deposits of oil that exist deep underground. Geologists take samples of rocks in several locations and examine them. They use their knowledge of how oil and rocks form to propose theories about the history of a location. They then narrow the possible locations to determine the best spots to drill.

Directions: Write three things you learned from reading the fluency passage.

1. I learned _____

_____

2. I learned _____

_____

3. I learned _____

_____

Unit 17
Science

Activity 1

Lesson
5

Think-Pair-Share

Name _____ Date _____

Directions

Use the Think-Pair-Share Strategy to complete the question below.

Step 1: **Think** about the question for one minute.

Step 2: **Pair** and complete the question with your partner.

Step 3: **Share** what you wrote with the class.

Create

Suppose you're a seismologist who predicts that an earthquake of intense magnitude will soon strike your area. Use your knowledge of the Mercalli intensity scale to *create* a bulletin notifying people about necessary preparations and essential supplies they'll need to survive the earthquake.

Fluency Practice: Decoding Multipart Words

Name _____ Date _____

Hurricane Katrina

Hurricanes pose a great danger to people who live near ocean coasts. The winds and waves of hurricanes can be very destructive as they come ashore. Hurricane Katrina struck the Gulf Coast of the United States in 2005 with deadly force. It was the costliest hurricane ever to hit the United States, doing more than $80 billion in damage and taking more than eighteen hundred lives.

The strength of Hurricane Katrina was only one of the factors that made it so deadly. The hurricane touched land in Florida before traveling back into the Gulf of Mexico. Hurricanes generally lose energy when they move onto land. Katrina caused some damage in Florida but was not especially strong there, ranking only as a Category 1 storm. However, when the hurricane moved back into the warm waters of the gulf, it gained tremendous strength and became a powerful storm. Warm ocean currents increase the power of hurricanes. Hurricane Katrina became a Category 3 storm. At times, Katrina surged to become a Category 5 hurricane, the most powerful kind.

Katrina then struck land in Louisiana and Mississippi. The most extensive damage took place in New Orleans, a highly populated city that was not built to withstand the flooding caused by Katrina. The storm surges were so strong they broke through the levees built to keep floodwaters out. After the levees were destroyed, water poured into New Orleans and flooded many sections of the city.

Other cities also suffered damage from Katrina. Mobile, Alabama, and Gulfport, Mississippi, were two cities hit especially hard. Hurricane Katrina moved through the entire state of Mississippi, doing so much damage that all eighty-two counties were declared disaster areas.

People from all over the United States and the rest of the world worked to help those who had lost their homes to Katrina. Communities sponsored families, finding jobs and homes for them. Former presidents Bill Clinton and George H. W. Bush headed a fund-raising campaign to rebuild New Orleans.

Fluency Practice: Standardized Test

Name _____ Date _____

Hurricane Katrina

Hurricanes pose a great danger to people who live near ocean coasts. The winds and waves of hurricanes can be very destructive as they come ashore. Hurricane Katrina struck the Gulf Coast of the United States in 2005 with deadly force. It was the costliest hurricane ever to hit the United States, doing more than $80 billion in damage and taking more than eighteen hundred lives.

The strength of Hurricane Katrina was only one of the factors that made it so deadly. The hurricane touched land in Florida before traveling back into the Gulf of Mexico. Hurricanes generally lose energy when they move onto land. Katrina caused some damage in Florida but was not especially strong there, ranking only as a Category 1 storm. However, when the hurricane moved back into the warm waters of the gulf, it gained tremendous strength and became a powerful storm. Warm ocean currents increase the power of hurricanes. Hurricane Katrina became a Category 3 storm. At times, Katrina surged to become a Category 5 hurricane, the most powerful kind.

Katrina then struck land in Louisiana and Mississippi. The most extensive damage took place in New Orleans, a highly populated city that was not built to withstand the flooding caused by Katrina. The storm surges were so strong they broke through the levees built to keep floodwaters out. After the levees were destroyed, water poured into New Orleans and flooded many sections of the city.

Other cities also suffered damage from Katrina. Mobile, Alabama, and Gulfport, Mississippi, were two cities hit especially hard. Hurricane Katrina moved through the entire state of Mississippi, doing so much damage that all eighty-two counties were declared disaster areas.

People from all over the United States and the rest of the world worked to help those who had lost their homes to Katrina. Communities sponsored families, finding jobs and homes for them. Former presidents Bill Clinton and George H. W. Bush headed a fund-raising campaign to rebuild New Orleans.

Score _____ /8 = _____ %

Directions: Take turns reading the questions. Answer the questions together.

| Level 1: "Remember" Questions—each worth 1 point |

For Level 1 questions, fill in the space next to the correct answer in your own Workbook.

1. Where are hurricanes most dangerous to people and their homes?
   ○ a. Near lakes   ○ c. Near coasts
   ○ b. By plateaus   ○ d. More inland

Fluency Practice: Standardized Test, continued

Name _____ Date _____

2. What usually happens when a hurricane moves onto land?
   ○ a. The hurricane's winds get stronger.
   ○ b. The hurricane loses energy.
   ○ c. Temperatures rise in surrounding areas.
   ○ d. Severe thunderstorms develop.

3. Hurricane Katrina gained tremendous strength when it moved back into
   ○ a. warm ocean currents.   ○ c. precipitation.
   ○ b. warm air temperatures.   ○ d. upward drafts.

4. Where did Hurricane Katrina do the most extensive damage?
   ○ a. Birmingham, Alabama   ○ c. Miami, Florida
   ○ b. Shreveport, Louisiana   ○ d. New Orleans, Louisiana

5. Which state had damage in all eighty-two counties?
   ○ a. Louisiana   ○ c. Florida
   ○ b. Mississippi   ○ d. Georgia

6. Which two presidents raised money to help those affected by Katrina?
   ○ a. Bill Clinton and George H.W. Bush
   ○ b. Jimmy Carter and Ronald Reagan
   ○ c. Ronald Reagan and Bill Clinton
   ○ d. Jimmy Carter and George H.W. Bush

Level 2: "Understand" Question—worth 2 points (2 points for correct answer, 1 point for partially correct answer, 0 points for incorrect answer)

For the Level 2 question, write the answer in the space provided in your own Workbook.

7. Explain the progress of Katrina from the time it initially hit land to when it became a powerful and destructive hurricane.

   _____

   _____

   _____

   _____

   _____

Fluency Practice: Information Learned

Name _____ Date _____

Hurricane Katrina

Hurricanes pose a great danger to people who live near ocean coasts. The winds and waves of hurricanes can be very destructive as they come ashore. Hurricane Katrina struck the Gulf Coast of the United States in 2005 with deadly force. It was the costliest hurricane ever to hit the United States, doing more than $80 billion in damage and taking more than eighteen hundred lives.

The strength of Hurricane Katrina was only one of the factors that made it so deadly. The hurricane touched land in Florida before traveling back into the Gulf of Mexico. Hurricanes generally lose energy when they move onto land. Katrina caused some damage in Florida but was not especially strong there, ranking only as a Category 1 storm. However, when the hurricane moved back into the warm waters of the gulf, it gained tremendous strength and became a powerful storm. Warm ocean currents increase the power of hurricanes. Hurricane Katrina became a Category 3 storm. At times, Katrina surged to become a Category 5 hurricane, the most powerful kind.

Katrina then struck land in Louisiana and Mississippi. The most extensive damage took place in New Orleans, a highly populated city that was not built to withstand the flooding caused by Katrina. The storm surges were so strong they broke through the levees built to keep floodwaters out. After the levees were destroyed, water poured into New Orleans and flooded many sections of the city.

Other cities also suffered damage from Katrina. Mobile, Alabama, and Gulfport, Mississippi, were two cities hit especially hard. Hurricane Katrina moved through the entire state of Mississippi, doing so much damage that all eighty-two counties were declared disaster areas.

People from all over the United States and the rest of the world worked to help those who had lost their homes to Katrina. Communities sponsored families, finding jobs and homes for them. Former presidents Bill Clinton and George H. W. Bush headed a fund-raising campaign to rebuild New Orleans.

Fluency Practice: Decoding Multipart Words

Name _____ Date _____

The Mariana Trench

The deepest location on Earth is at the bottom of the Pacific Ocean in an area known as the Mariana Trench. This trench is located just east of the Mariana Islands, which are southeast of Japan. Approximately 6.8 miles below the surface, the Mariana Trench is cold and dark. The extreme depth produces intense pressure a thousand times the air pressure we experience on Earth's surface. Without protective equipment, humans could not survive in the Mariana Trench.

However, you might be surprised to learn that life does exist in the Mariana Trench. Despite the extreme conditions, these ocean depths are home to some interesting fish, crabs, and other animals. These organisms must live and find food in total darkness. Many organisms, such as the anglerfish, provide their own light. One surprising characteristic of organisms found in the trench is that they often live much longer than surface organisms. Many of the fish live more than a hundred years.

Not all parts of the Mariana Trench are cold. Hydrothermal vents can be found in various locations along the trench. These vents discharge heat from deep within Earth, which can cause water temperatures to rise as high as 572 degrees Fahrenheit! As you might guess, there are thriving communities of life in the warm areas near these thermal vents.

Using many technological developments, humans have been able to visit the Mariana Trench and explore it. A Swiss scientist named Jacques Piccard, along with U.S. Navy Lieutenant Don Walsh, first explored the trench in 1960 in a submarine developed by Piccard's father. The two men descended 35,810 feet to the ocean floor, the deepest dive in history. Until Piccard explored the trench, scientists doubted that life could exist under the extreme conditions there. In 1995, Japanese scientists sent robots into the trench to do extensive exploration, take pictures, and extract samples for testing. The scientists found that mud samples from the bottom contained a wide variety of bacteria. They also learned that many organisms, such as shrimp, sea cucumbers, and worms, live on the ocean floor in the trench.

Fluency Practice: Standardized Test

Name _____ Date _____

The Mariana Trench

The deepest location on Earth is at the bottom of the Pacific Ocean in an area known as the Mariana Trench. This trench is located just east of the Mariana Islands, which are southeast of Japan. Approximately 6.8 miles below the surface, the Mariana Trench is cold and dark. The extreme depth produces intense pressure a thousand times the air pressure we experience on Earth's surface. Without protective equipment, humans could not survive in the Mariana Trench.

However, you might be surprised to learn that life does exist in the Mariana Trench. Despite the extreme conditions, these ocean depths are home to some interesting fish, crabs, and other animals. These organisms must live and find food in total darkness. Many organisms, such as the anglerfish, provide their own light. One surprising characteristic of organisms found in the trench is that they often live much longer than surface organisms. Many of the fish live more than a hundred years.

Not all parts of the Mariana Trench are cold. Hydrothermal vents can be found in various locations along the trench. These vents discharge heat from deep within Earth, which can cause water temperatures to rise as high as 572 degrees Fahrenheit! As you might guess, there are thriving communities of life in the warm areas near these thermal vents.

Using many technological developments, humans have been able to visit the Mariana Trench and explore it. A Swiss scientist named Jacques Piccard, along with U.S. Navy Lieutenant Don Walsh, first explored the trench in 1960 in a submarine developed by Piccard's father. The two men descended 35,810 feet to the ocean floor, the deepest dive in history. Until Piccard explored the trench, scientists doubted that life could exist under the extreme conditions there. In 1995, Japanese scientists sent robots into the trench to do extensive exploration, take pictures, and extract samples for testing. The scientists found that mud samples from the bottom contained a wide variety of bacteria. They also learned that many organisms, such as shrimp, sea cucumbers, and worms, live on the ocean floor in the trench.

Score _____ /8 = _____ %

Directions: Take turns reading the questions. Answer the questions together.

Level 1: "Remember" Questions—each worth 1 point

For Level 1 questions, fill in the space next to the correct answer in your own Workbook.

1. In which ocean is the Mariana Trench?
- ○ a. Atlantic Ocean
- ○ b. Pacific Ocean
- ○ c. Indian Ocean
- ○ d. Arctic Ocean

Lesson
3

Fluency Practice: Standardized Test, continued

Name _____ Date _____

2. In addition to not being able to breathe, why couldn't humans survive in the Mariana Trench?
   - ○ a. The extreme depth produces pressures that are too intense.
   - ○ b. The extreme depth ensures there isn't enough food available.
   - ○ c. The extreme depth produces water temperatures that are too cold.
   - ○ d. The extreme depth creates subduction zones that are constantly shifting.

3. The organisms in the Mariana Trench must live and find food
   - ○ a. with netting structures they have in their bodies.
   - ○ b. with the bit of sunlight that makes it down that far.
   - ○ c. near the surface of the ocean.
   - ○ d. in total darkness.

4. What is one surprising thing about the organisms found in the trench?
   - ○ a. Many have specialized fins to swim to the surface.
   - ○ b. Many live more than a hundred years.
   - ○ c. Many are mammals.
   - ○ d. Many are very dangerous to humans.

5. How hot can water temperatures get around hydrothermal vents along the trench?
   - ○ a. 100 degrees Fahrenheit   ○ c. 572 degrees Fahrenheit
   - ○ b. 775 degrees Fahrenheit   ○ d. 272 degrees Fahrenheit

6. Who was the first to explore the Mariana Trench in 1960?
   - ○ a. Jacques Cousteau   ○ c. Jacques Piccard
   - ○ b. John Steele   ○ d. William Beebe

Level 2: "Understand" Question—worth 2 points (2 points for correct answer, 1 point for partially correct answer, 0 points for incorrect answer)

For the Level 2 question, write the answer in the space provided in your own Workbook.

7. Explain how technology has helped humans visit and explore the Mariana Trench.

_____

_____

_____

_____

_____

Fluency Practice: Information Learned

Name _____ Date _____

The Mariana Trench

The deepest location on Earth is at the bottom of the Pacific Ocean in an area known as the Mariana Trench. This trench is located just east of the Mariana Islands, which are southeast of Japan. Approximately 6.8 miles below the surface, the Mariana Trench is cold and dark. The extreme depth produces intense pressure a thousand times the air pressure we experience on Earth's surface. Without protective equipment, humans could not survive in the Mariana Trench.

However, you might be surprised to learn that life does exist in the Mariana Trench. Despite the extreme conditions, these ocean depths are home to some interesting fish, crabs, and other animals. These organisms must live and find food in total darkness. Many organisms, such as the anglerfish, provide their own light. One surprising characteristic of organisms found in the trench is that they often live much longer than surface organisms. Many of the fish live more than a hundred years.

Not all parts of the Mariana Trench are cold. Hydrothermal vents can be found in various locations along the trench. These vents discharge heat from deep within Earth, which can cause water temperatures to rise as high as 572 degrees Fahrenheit! As you might guess, there are thriving communities of life in the warm areas near these thermal vents.

Using many technological developments, humans have been able to visit the Mariana Trench and explore it. A Swiss scientist named Jacques Piccard, along with U.S. Navy Lieutenant Don Walsh, first explored the trench in 1960 in a submarine developed by Piccard's father. The two men descended 35,810 feet to the ocean floor, the deepest dive in history. Until Piccard explored the trench, scientists doubted that life could exist under the extreme conditions there. In 1995, Japanese scientists sent robots into the trench to do extensive exploration, take pictures, and extract samples for testing. The scientists found that mud samples from the bottom contained a wide variety of bacteria. They also learned that many organisms, such as shrimp, sea cucumbers, and worms, live on the ocean floor in the trench.

Lesson 2

Fluency Practice: Decoding Multipart Words

Name _____ Date _____

Mars: Planet of Mystery

For centuries, Mars has been shrouded in more mystery than any other planet. Humans have long wondered if life exists, or ever existed, on Mars. Mars is close enough to Earth that for a long time humans have been able to examine it through telescopes. The red surface of Mars seems a mysterious place. The concept of alien life was expressed in popular culture in 1898 when H. G. Wells wrote *The War of the Worlds,* a book in which Martians attack Earth. In the 1940s, Ray Bradbury wrote *The Martian Chronicles,* which describes a planet inhabited by a society of Martians.

Some of Bradbury's visions were observed by the first few space missions that explored Mars. In 1971, two Soviet space probes landed on Mars, but both probes immediately lost contact with Earth. Eerily, a similar scenario in Bradbury's novel details Martian efforts to sabotage Earth probes. Years later, the mysteries mounted when the first Viking probe flew over Mars, photographing the surface. One of the pictures seemed to show a large landform with the features of a human face.

In 1976, NASA successfully landed the *Viking 1* and *Viking 2* explorer probes on Mars's surface. These probes were operational for several years and transmitted beautiful color pictures to Earth. None of the pictures, however, showed any traces of Martians or any other life-forms. Even the infamous Mars "face" was discovered to be just a group of ordinary mountains casting a shadow.

Ironically, after so many years, there is now some evidence that suggests life may exist or may once have existed on Mars. However, the life is not as exciting or as scary as Bradbury's aliens. It consists of microscopic organisms. The main evidence comes from a meteorite that supposedly came from Mars. The meteorite contains compounds that could have come from organisms. In addition, current Mars probes have revealed traces of methane, a by-product of living things. Information from the probes has also confirmed that, sometime in the past, there was water on Mars.

Lesson 3

Fluency Practice: Standardized Test

Name _____ Date _____

Mars: Planet of Mystery

For centuries, Mars has been shrouded in more mystery than any other planet. Humans have long wondered if life exists, or ever existed, on Mars. Mars is close enough to Earth that for a long time humans have been able to examine it through telescopes. The red surface of Mars seems a mysterious place. The concept of alien life was expressed in popular culture in 1898 when H. G. Wells wrote *The War of the Worlds,* a book in which Martians attack Earth. In the 1940s, Ray Bradbury wrote *The Martian Chronicles,* which describes a planet inhabited by a society of Martians.

Some of Bradbury's visions were observed by the first few space missions that explored Mars. In 1971, two Soviet space probes landed on Mars, but both probes immediately lost contact with Earth. Eerily, a similar scenario in Bradbury's novel details Martian efforts to sabotage Earth probes. Years later, the mysteries mounted when the first Viking probe flew over Mars, photographing the surface. One of the pictures seemed to show a large landform with the features of a human face.

In 1976, NASA successfully landed the *Viking 1* and *Viking 2* explorer probes on Mars's surface. These probes were operational for several years and transmitted beautiful color pictures to Earth. None of the pictures, however, showed any traces of Martians or any other life-forms. Even the infamous Mars "face" was discovered to be just a group of ordinary mountains casting a shadow.

Ironically, after so many years, there is now some evidence that suggests life may exist or may once have existed on Mars. However, the life is not as exciting or as scary as Bradbury's aliens. It consists of microscopic organisms. The main evidence comes from a meteorite that supposedly came from Mars. The meteorite contains compounds that could have come from organisms. In addition, current Mars probes have revealed traces of methane, a by-product of living things. Information from the probes has also confirmed that, sometime in the past, there was water on Mars.

Score _____ /8 = _____ %

Directions: Take turns reading the questions. Answer the questions together.

Level 1: "Remember" Questions—each worth 1 point

For Level 1 questions, fill in the space next to the correct answer in your own Workbook.

1. If you looked through a telescope at Mars's surface, what color would you see?
- ◯ a. White
- ◯ b. Orange
- ◯ c. Red
- ◯ d. Blue

Lesson

3

Fluency Practice: Standardized Test, continued

Name _____ Date _____

2. Who wrote *The War of the Worlds* in 1898?
   ○ a. Ray Bradbury   ○ c. H. G. Wells
   ○ b. George Orwell   ○ d. J. R. R. Tolkien

3. What year did Soviet space probes first land on Mars?
   ○ a. 1969   ○ c. 1981
   ○ b. 1971   ○ d. 1975

4. One picture taken of Mars's surface seemed to show a large land feature with
   ○ a. an ancient city around it.
   ○ b. a dried-up lake bed.
   ○ c. trees surrounding it.
   ○ d. the shape of a human face.

5. What were *Viking 1* and *Viking 2*?
   ○ a. Stars   ○ c. Moons
   ○ b. Space shuttles   ○ d. Probes

6. What type of life may exist on Mars?
   ○ a. Microscopic organisms   ○ c. Green plants
   ○ b. Small mammals   ○ d. Desert animals

Level 2: "Understand" Question—worth 2 points (2 points for correct answer, 1 point for partially correct answer, 0 points for incorrect answer)

For the Level 2 question, write the answer in the space provided in your own Workbook.

7. Describe the evidence that suggests life may exist or may once have existed on Mars.

_____

_____

_____

_____

_____

_____

Fluency Practice: Information Learned

Name _____ Date _____

Mars: Planet of Mystery

For centuries, Mars has been shrouded in more mystery than any other planet. Humans have long wondered if life exists, or ever existed, on Mars. Mars is close enough to Earth that for a long time humans have been able to examine it through telescopes. The red surface of Mars seems a mysterious place. The concept of alien life was expressed in popular culture in 1898 when H. G. Wells wrote *The War of the Worlds,* a book in which Martians attack Earth. In the 1940s, Ray Bradbury wrote *The Martian Chronicles,* which describes a planet inhabited by a society of Martians.

Some of Bradbury's visions were observed by the first few space missions that explored Mars. In 1971, two Soviet space probes landed on Mars, but both probes immediately lost contact with Earth. Eerily, a similar scenario in Bradbury's novel details Martian efforts to sabotage Earth probes. Years later, the mysteries mounted when the first Viking probe flew over Mars, photographing the surface. One of the pictures seemed to show a large landform with the features of a human face.

In 1976, NASA successfully landed the *Viking 1* and *Viking 2* explorer probes on Mars's surface. These probes were operational for several years and transmitted beautiful color pictures to Earth. None of the pictures, however, showed any traces of Martians or any other life-forms. Even the infamous Mars "face" was discovered to be just a group of ordinary mountains casting a shadow.

Ironically, after so many years, there is now some evidence that suggests life may exist or may once have existed on Mars. However, the life is not as exciting or as scary as Bradbury's aliens. It consists of microscopic organisms. The main evidence comes from a meteorite that supposedly came from Mars. The meteorite contains compounds that could have come from organisms. In addition, current Mars probes have revealed traces of methane, a by-product of living things. Information from the probes has also confirmed that, sometime in the past, there was water on Mars.

Fluency Chart

Name _____

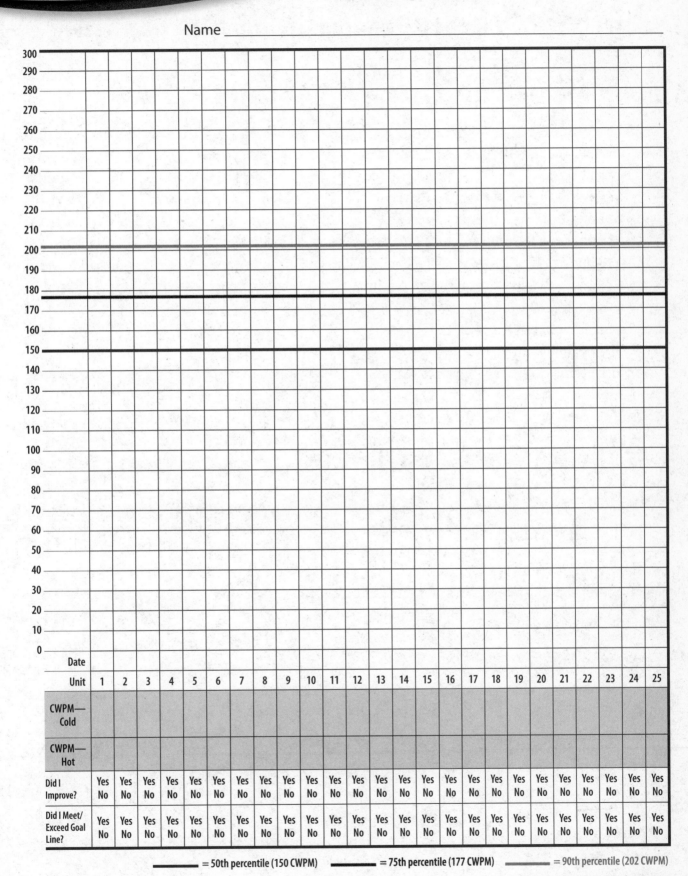

		1	2	3	4	5	6	7	8	9	10	11	12	13	14	15	16	17	18	19	20	21	22	23	24	25
Date																										
Unit		1	2	3	4	5	6	7	8	9	10	11	12	13	14	15	16	17	18	19	20	21	22	23	24	25
CWPM— Cold																										
CWPM— Hot																										
Did I Improve?		Yes No	Yes No	Yes No	Yes No	Yes No	Yes No	Yes No	Yes No	Yes No	Yes No	Yes No	Yes No	Yes No	Yes No	Yes No	Yes No	Yes No	Yes No	Yes No	Yes No	Yes No	Yes No	Yes No	Yes No	Yes No
Did I Meet/ Exceed Goal Line?		Yes No	Yes No	Yes No	Yes No	Yes No	Yes No	Yes No	Yes No	Yes No	Yes No	Yes No	Yes No	Yes No	Yes No	Yes No	Yes No	Yes No	Yes No	Yes No	Yes No	Yes No	Yes No	Yes No	Yes No	Yes No

———— = 50th percentile (150 CWPM)   ———— = 75th percentile (177 CWPM)   ———— = 90th percentile (202 CWPM)